Contents

CENTER FOR CREATIVE PHOTOGRAPHY is a research publication of previously unpublished or unique material from the collections in the archives of the Center for Creative Photography. Subscription and renewal rate: $20 (USA), $25 (foreign) for five issues. Back issues available. Address inquiries and subscriptions to: Center for Creative Photography, University of Arizona, 843 East University Boulevard, Tucson, Arizona 85719.

This publication is supported by a grant from the
National Endowment for the Arts, a federal agency.

BACK COVER:
W. EUGENE SMITH: untitled, ca. 1935.
(Note on back of photograph: "1931 Chevy stalled
at edge of flood that destroyed McCooke Bridge
near Wichita, Kansas, ca. 1935.
Friend Edward Armstrong in car.")

FRONT COVER:
"W. Eugene Smith aboard the U.S.S. Bunker Hill, 1943."
Photographer unknown.

Director's Statement

THIS ISSUE OF THE CENTER'S PUBLICATION is devoted to a selection of W. Eugene Smith's early photographs, the majority of which have never been published or seen before by the public or scholars. A few of the images have appeared in print only in the original periodicals for which they were produced between 1939 and 1951. Even with the publication of this portfolio of 99 images, less than ten percent of Smith's masterworks in the Center's archive will have been presented for appreciation and evaluation. This simply means that the research and study of W. Eugene Smith as an artist has barely begun, and that one of the Center's priorities will be to aid scholars and students in a thorough and complete investigation of Smith and his work over the coming years. In addition to unknown images, the Smith archive also contains an unsurpassed number of often unique examples of Smith's most well known photographs.

The attending materials in the archive such as negatives, contact sheets, correspondence, and notes provide an unequaled opportunity, as do each of the Center's archives, to study personal attitudes and working methods in relation to finished works. All too often written history must depend to a certain extent upon contemporary conjecture of personal motives in relation to a surviving fact or object, not to mention the sorely tested temptation of both criticism and history to make the evidence fit the theory. Archives such as the W. Eugene Smith collection should substantially lessen the potential for such problems, while providing at the same time documentation for an increased consideration of the humanity surrounding a work of art.

I wish to express gratitude to Mr. John Morris who has written for this issue a personal remembrance of his lifelong friendship and working relationship with Smith. The closeness of that relationship is reflected in Smith's designation before his death of Mr. Morris as executor of his estate. I also wish to acknowledge the tremendous organizational effort and months of research which William Johnson devoted to the Smith archive in order to make this publication possible. As a result of his research he has written a fine essay on Smith's early career in photography and compiled the most extensive Smith bibliography to date. This issue of the Center's publication includes the first half of the bibliography which pertains to the years covered by the portfolio and the essay. The remainder of the bibliography will be published as a supplement to a future issue of the Center's publication.

This issue is, of course, substantially larger than most issues of our publication, as was the previous issue devoted to Margrethe Mather. In both cases a grant from the National Endowment for the Arts made the expanded format possible. While such sizeable issues will remain the goal for our publications based on outside funding and subsidies, they will also remain exceptions within the series.

Finally, I would like to express appreciation to Minnette Burges, Publications Coordinator, who guided this complex issue of our publication through production to completion.

JAMES L. ENYEART

3

AUTHOR'S NOTE

ONE OF THE CRUCIAL ASPECTS of W. Eugene Smith's art and of his public career was his insistence that his was not an art of brilliant individual photographs but an art of the coherent photo-essay. His insistence on the rights and responsibilities of the photographer to control the form of the presentation of his own photographs is part of Smith's history and part of Smith's legend.

During his lifetime, Smith was never able to publish the full photo essays as he photographed them and therefore the largest portion of his photographs are not known. Once all the published and unpublished photographs in the W. Eugene Smith Archive at the Center for Creative Photography were drawn together and seen as a body of work several facts became apparent. First, the "known" (i.e. published) Smith images are a tiny fraction of the total body of his excellent work. In other words, Smith did not make a few dozen "beautiful" photographs and thousands of indifferent photographs. Smith made many hundreds of "beautiful" photographs — many of which have never been seen publicly.

The work of art for Smith was the essay, and not any particular images within it. Obviously, some essays are far more extended and/or successful than others, but he very seldom thought in terms of the "single" image; and the number of "isolated" images in his work is tiny in comparison to the size of his oeuvre.

Smith did have a highly developed narrative sense and he could put together numbers of images around a particular topic in a manner that was coherent, meaningful, and expressive. This means that he could take photographs of the grand landscape and of the telling detail, as well as photographs of the particulars of events and actions that were played out in the space between those two extremes. The groups of photographs that Smith chose to enlarge and mount from his total collection of negatives on any particular topic do usually constitute a powerfully expressive comment upon that topic. For major essays, he often enlarged and mounted several hundred photographs to represent his conception of that essay. It was not unusual for Smith to consider many cropping variations and many lay-out designs for each of his essays. The amount of materials that remains in the Archive demonstrates that he had spent hundreds of hours in careful painstaking assessment of many of the possible variations of presentation of each essay.

When I mention a particular photo-essay in this article I usually reference the published version of that essay. However, my comments are based on the experience of the larger, more comprehensive, and (in my opinion) greater essay that Smith, himself, put together.

W. J.

4

W. Eugene Smith: 1938-1951

by William Johnson

IN THE LATE 1930s the United States was coming out of the deepest economic depression in its history. And, while pockets of distress and chaos still existed, the country was filled with a brawling sense of energy. The sudden explosion into publication of large-size picture magazines shared and reflected that energy. *Life*'s instant and amazing popular success was quickly followed by a flood of similar publications such as *Look, Flash!, Focus, Foto, Click, Ken, Pic, Pictures, See,* and others which soon launched into print.

These brash, raw, democratic and extraordinarily vital magazines were packed with hundreds of photographs — photographs of anything and everything. Political turmoil in the Far East, a chorine's make-up secrets, the latest discoveries of science — all were held up to the public's entranced gaze.

An avid reader, (or perhaps more accurately an avid looker) could probably see well over a thousand photographs each month.[1] These illustrated magazines were also taking on a new dimension in the general social structures within the country. They were picking up a certain energy — becoming "hot" — and were evolving into forceful agencies within the social matrix that they reported upon. Very quickly *Life* photographers and others would command attention, cooperation and even obedience from the world that they reported about. It was an active scene, filled with the potential for change and expansion. The role of the photojournalist was altering, his social status shifting from minor craftsman to media star.

Under these pressures, the vocabulary that defined the style of traditional news photography began to flux and shift. Previously, the rigorous commitment to present the subject as information, coupled to the limitations of the awkward, cumbersome press cameras then available, had produced a direct record style. Subject was all — its presentation as simple as possible. One aspect of change was the injection of the style of commercial photography into the previously mundane news photograph. And style in the best commercial photography of the day was a high style, aspiring to art and flavored with the spice of European Constructivism spun out in the abrupt, angular, crisp, and above all "modern" presentations of the "New-Objectivity" movement of the 1920s. The best commercial photographers using this style in this country were Edward Steichen, Anton Bruehl, Paul Outerbridge and Martin Munkacsi. Much of the photography in these new magazines was dynamic, exciting, and filled with the movement necessary to catch the eye and hold the attention.

Margaret Bourke-White, a younger photographer who displayed this mix of formal interest and newsworthy subject in her early work, developed into one of photojournalism's "stars" of that decade. An even younger photographer named W. Eugene Smith also presented photographs of mingled crispness and action that soon attracted attention with their technical perfection, beautiful composition and sense of movement. An admirer of Martin Munkacsi, Smith was skilled, eager and active. His talent was obvious, his energy amazing and his enthusiasm was infectious. By the time he was twenty-one, he was successful and, moreover, beginning to be discussed with wonder by his peers.[2]

Smith began photographing while at his Wichita, Kansas high school in the early thirties. He worked part-time for the Wichita newspapers and in 1934, when he was 16, his photographs of the drought appeared in the *New York Times*. By the time he had graduated from high school he was already fixed on a photographic career. After six months at the University of Notre Dame, where he made some 1,400 photographs, the initial publication of *Life* drew him to New York. Very quickly he began to work as a news photographer. His first job for *Newsweek* was brief and from late 1938 through 1943

Se, Sept. 8–12, 1939.

he worked as a freelance photographer associated with the Black Star Photo agency. It was a time of hectic activity, enormous energy, and immediate success for Smith. Within two years his work was published with more than fifty articles in the United States, Canada, South America and Europe.

This work often appeared as a single image or as a small group of photographs loosely clustered around a simple theme. The nature of the assignments and the format of the publications prevented a coherent focus in his work and the dominant strength in his early work is the sense of vitality and technical skill that was displayed within the individual images. Taken as a group, however, a very large and complex body of work was made during this period. It was claimed that he made approximately 50,000 negatives before World War II.[3]

In 1939, he signed a retainer contract to work for two weeks out of each month for *Life*. While working for *Life* conferred enormous prestige and must have provided Smith with a strong feeling of satisfaction, the work in itself was rather limiting, consisting primarily of single images or minor essays. During 1941, Smith was allowed a slightly broader scope of action and he began to produce a few larger stories such as "Prisons Turn to Sports Programs," (*Life,* May 5, 1941) and "Women's Prisons," (*Life,* Oct. 6, 1941). However, these stories were still relatively minor and were often mixed with smaller, sporadic assignments. After the initial flush of excitement from actually working at *Life* had faded, Smith seems to have soon grown restless with the limitations of his duties there.

From 1940 to 1942, the work Smith produced for *American Magazine* and, in particular, *Colliers Magazine,* was, in a sense, more coherent than that at *Life* magazine. In fact, Smith seems to have become almost a de facto staff photographer for *Colliers* during 1941 and 1942, producing photographs for that magazine almost weekly. The limitation with this arrangement was that *Colliers* most frequently used only one, or at best a very few photographs for each article. These photographs were used primarily as illustrations to the *Colliers* texts and seldom conveyed much weight or meaning within themselves. Also, the nature of the articles illustrated were often rather mundane, topical, trivial and ultimately irritating to Smith.

Colliers, March 7, 1942.

At this point, probably frustrated with his junior status at *Life,* and certainly becoming dissatisfied with the authoritarian structure of that magazine, Smith quit *Life* in 1941. In a short time, he began to work for the newly established weekly magazine *Parade.*

Smith stated to me in conversation that his time at *Parade* was a happy time for him, and that it was there that he learned how to put together a coherent photo essay. The facts seem to belie the second half of the statement, as he had already produced a number of coherent stories for *Life* and *Colliers.* Nevertheless, it may have been that at *Parade* he sensed more of the creative possibilities that the photographer had within the context of making a photo story. And he certainly had a much finer forum for the display of his work, since he was able to publish an extended number of fifteen to twenty photographs on one subject, well displayed almost bi-weekly in a five or six page layout in 1942 and during the first part of 1943.

During the first few years of its existence, *Parade* magazine used photography much more frequently and with a much greater emphasis than it does today. A typical issue would contain one or two extended "narrative" photo stories of ten to twenty photographs and the remainder of the space was filled with shorter photo stories or single images.

More so than many of the other magazines, *Parade* accepted a very high level of manipulation of its feature stories. These stories were frequently, in effect, short narrative still picture "film scripts" usually based on a theoretical "real life" situation. A story concept would be written and blocked out by an editor, often professional models would be hired, and on occasion even exact shot angles would be worked out before the photographer went to the location. The photographs would then be edited, as if they were a film, for maximum visual impact, narrative coherency, and dramatic presentation.

At *Parade,* Smith learned to vary his photographic stance in order to develop his vocabulary of images, firm up his pacing, and increase his

7

Parade, July 5, 1942.

skill at photographing a larger body of action or a more complex subject with greater ease and flexibility. It is here that Smith developed and certainly refined the acute narrative sensibility that would take him through the remainder of his career.

During the later half of the 1930s, the documentary idea was the most forceful ideological concept fermenting the mix from which an artist works to produce his own individual statements of value. A major concept embedded in the documentary idea is that it is the function of art to inform and instruct, and that thus it functions as a ligature in the social fabric. At the depth of the Depression, a major message of documentary photography had been that the poor, the dispossessed, and the disenfranchised were also human beings and that they were also a valuable part of the social fabric. An ideology of the value of the common man was affirmed and while a focus was placed on the hardships caused to the poor by the economic and social dislocations that were in play during the period, the documentary movement, for the most part, did not offer clearcut ideological or political solutions to these problems. Most often the emphasis rested on a broad humanistic belief in the democratic process.

The young photographer W. Eugene Smith inherited and accepted this tradition in art. He would foster and further this belief through his entire life and within his entire career.

Soon after 1936 the ominous mushrooming of totalitarian ideologies, backed by increasingly belligerent and powerful governments overseas and by growing random groups at home, fed a need for the self-focusing of ideals in this country. The media restressed the role of the "common man," defined and articulated his position and value in the social fabric, and outlined the

American Magazine, April, 1939.

beliefs and values of the democratic form of government. While the news media and popular magazines continued to report on such traditional subjects as politicians and political affairs, celebrities, "society," sports figures, and the bizarre with its usual gusto, it also began to display an incessant and consuming interest in the daily affairs of Everyman. *Life*'s focusing on "life," the *American Magazine*'s monthly series "Interesting People in the American Scene" — with its golfers, baton twirlers, delivery truck drivers, safe crackers, horticulturists, etc. — typify this position. Together, the stories created the idea of a complex, detailed, and interlocking society of interesting individuals freely engaged in activities of their own choice.

In the early 1940s virtually all of the mass magazines, even those such as *Friday* and *Look* which previously had been isolationist or pacifist, supported the impending war effort. These magazines developed an idealized display of this nation as a country of might tempered by reasoned justice. The United States was reaffirming for itself the concept that it was the "Bulwark of Democracy" for the world.

The magazines developed a rhetoric of energetic confidence to convey those ideas and a photographic style which manifested those ideals began to be favored. American war propaganda was in a curiously difficult position. The nation was preparing to fight a war to defend the rights of the individual — and as such the propagandists were placed in the ironic situation of calling on individuals to give up those rights, even to the point of giving up their life for "the greater good," in order that they meet their social obligations. This uneasy balance between the individual and his social function was the ideological area that American propaganda had to work within.

During the early 1940s, *Parade*'s editorial policy was to provide a high percentage of public service articles designed to explain the functions of various social agencies, groups, or programs to the broad reading public. Many articles were war-related — "Will the Farmer Win the War?", "Betty Watson is a Wave," "Training American Commandos." These articles often took the form of a tightly scripted narrative detailing the pertinent features of the chosen topic, as they were displayed through the actions of an individual. Thus by following First Sergeant James I. Crenshaw through his daily routine in "Portrait of a Top Sergeant" (*Parade*, Sept. 13, 1942), the reader would understand and identify with the nature and functions of his office. This

Colliers, May 30, 1942. (Original in color.)

specific top sergeant was presented as a unique individual and at the same time as a representative of all top sergeants. The act of personalizing social roles while at the same time dissolving the individual into a realm of abstraction often established an ironic dichotomy.

From 1941 to 1943, propelled by his own desire to support the war effort and structured by the nature of his assignments, Smith easily converted his energetic style to war propaganda efforts and his photographs were convincing and effective examples of this use of photography. Working at an even more hectic pace, Smith produced scores of photographs and photo stories for *Life*, *American Magazine, Colliers,* and *Parade* to assist the war effort.

But propaganda needs to present a clearly understandable ideal, even at the expense of ideas. The complexities that abound in any system are repressed, the system's faults are minimized and its strengths featured. An ideology and the style that conveys this ideology is rigidly presented through the prism of one particular stance. But Smith's loyalties were ultimately to humanism before nationalism and to art before advertisement. The first rifts between his personal belief systems and those that fueled the war effort began to appear at about this time. The crucial substance of Smith's public career, his moral stance on the uses of photojournalism and his powerful effect on the history of the medium had its beginnings here, in the complex and highly charged mood surrounding World War II. During this war he made moral choices in the face of conflicting and opposing ideologies; defined and defended beliefs about the nature and uses of his art, and eventually found the powerful, mature photographic style that conveyed those beliefs with clarity and force.

By 1943, Smith was locked in a dilemma. His energy, talents and ambition had brought him to the forefront of his field with incredible speed. He was working hard, making good money and seeing his photographs appearing everywhere. Yet while he was photographing such stories as "What the Army Drinks" or "Interesting People in the American Scene: He Puts his Friends to Sleep," the battles of Leningrad and Stalingrad were being fought, the Allies were fighting for control of the North Atlantic, and the invasion of North Africa was underway. In short, the great events of the world were taking place outside his reach. By 1943, the American news media had 370 reporters and 65 photographers with the armed forces overseas.[4] The sheer volume of this commitment was historically unprecedented. But Smith was not a part of these historic events. He was boiling with impatience to get to the action.

Finally, after months of frustration, Smith was able to obtain an assignment as a war correspondent for *Flying* magazine. He left for the Pacific theater in late 1943, where he was finally assigned aboard the aircraft carrier U.S.S. Bunker Hill.

Smith went to the Pacific theater with an idea and a high ambition. His ambition was to catch history with his camera. His idea was to write a book about his experiences. During his time on board the U.S.S. Bunker Hill he photographed, wrote many letters to his family (and occasionally to History as well), and kept an extensive, detailed day-to-day account of his experiences on the ship.[5] This book concept would suffer many alterations over the next two years and was never realized; but the idea of the book and the letters provide an index to the subtle but profound alterations that take place in Smith's thoughts and in his photographs during this crucial time. His ambition is stated in a letter written on his 25th birthday, December 30, 1943:

> The first quarter of a century of my life is history today. It has slipped away never to be reclaimed. . . . I lay on my bunk reviewing my life the entire of last night. My life from the moment of my beginning, photography, should have veered from the superfluous that I have poorly recorded, and should have been dedicated to making one part of a record of the tragically momentous years dating from around 1930. I should have religiously spent my entire effort in letting deep history fall before my lens. . . . The great tragedy of wasted time has been the years of the war, . . . I have no explanation to free my conscience of the guilt of not having thrown myself into our

own war — from the date of December 7th on. Why, why did I sit it out; what a fool.[6]

During the winter of 1943 Smith photographed the carrier, its crews and its activities. He also helped out the official camera crews and worked diligently to acquire the confidence and respect of his companions. Gradually he was able to organize the cooperation necessary for him to participate in a number of aerial sorties from the U.S.S. Bunker Hill. These photographs were made under extraordinarily difficult conditions from the fighter-bombers and the problems and flavor of danger honed Smith's sense of form to the finest edge. His early photographs on board the U.S.S. Bunker Hill were filled with the same stylized devices of the war-preparedness work: sharp, aggressive, high-keyed lighting, harsh contrast, and abrupt angles all provided a rhetoric of energy. But a difference exists within these photographs — for reality has filled in the gaps. The rhetoric of energy was replaced by the reality of power. One of the mightiest naval armadas in history gave an aura of veracity to Smith's energetic photographs. These photographs are dynamic, forcefully composed, beautifully articulated comments on the grim elegance of the machinery of war. More importantly, they had been made real by the weight of the U.S. Navy.

In a letter dated November 17, 1943, Smith mentioned a crucial decision that affected his style:

I have not posed one single picture since I have been out here. Those who know my usual stuff are going to be surprised and probably disappointed. But there is no other way to do it. So the stuff will lack to an extent that 'too perfect' composition that I ordinarily have. But it will also lack much of the DRAMA — of this I am afraid. But it can't be helped ...

Some will say that I am being forced to shoot on the fly, that the results will be far truer. But this is false, for the finished picture must have the mood of the surroundings and interpret them, translating them into the finished work. The stuff I am shooting is — so far — record shooting which contains nothing more — it has no soul. I MUST DEFEAT THAT OR BE DEFEATED. ... Sometimes I find the price of IDEALISM VERY HIGH.

In fact, the lessons that he had learned from commercial photography were displayed very strongly in these photographs. While Smith might have perceived a loosening of composition within the images, in fact they are still strongly dominated by a rigorous structure. They were also dominated by a more subtle necessity that is embedded within all the commercial photography of the day. During this period both commercial and news photography formally "presented" their subjects to the viewer. This photography was designed to attract attention, to force a pause in a busy viewer, and to display its message in a heightened and exaggeratedly clear sense. Commercial photography was designed to be singular in meaning, not pluralistic, complex, or subtle. Smith would never lose that sense of use of a photograph, but he would shatter and reform its context during the next years.

In 1943, Smith's photography was a photography of display. This photography sets up a crucially irrevocable distance between the subject and the viewer. Smith intuitively felt this distance and was searching for a way to overcome it. The best possible solution seemed to be to get physically closer. He stated this in a letter written on January 16, 1944:

Am on my last job with a carrier, for this isn't the war to cover — it isn't my war. It is much too soft and safe and clean. My pictures and my life in the last few months have been almost wasted, at least toward the editorial I want to write on this war. To have gone in with Marines at Tarawa, or to have been in the whole Russian War, I could have done my job then, but not with the niceties and the luxuries of the Navy. Oh sure, there is danger, but it is not overpowering dread of instant death day in and day out, minute by minute that is the lot of some — and I feel they are the ones who know the real meaning of war.... True I have seen my friends die, and have been close to it many times myself, but even their dying is cleaner and less pitiful out here. Had I gone in with the waves of boys at Tarawa at the start, you would have seen some of the great and brutal war pictures that really tell what war is.

For Smith, then, it was not a war of materials, tactics and strategy. He was not interested in the war of the generals. For him, it was a war of determined men in desperate situations and he wanted to become one of those men. But his time on the carrier had not been totally wasted for Smith because he had developed a sense of shared community with those men as he photographed them:

Dick was climbing slightly into his circle (over Engebi Island) when — 'A collision — two planes — TBF's — ' his tensioned voice broke in. 'I'm going to fly low over the wreck-age.' I swung back to the little windows and prepared to shoot whatever passed beneath. Not knowing what to expect except wreck-age of some kind — this wasn't cold shooting of an accident; I had been with this ship through every battle. I felt that I was not an outsider covering a story — I was part of that ship. Many of those people were the best friends I had in the world. I didn't know who was broken and lifeless in that wreckage down there but I knew it was going to be a burn into the soul....[7]

Once Smith established the sense of shared community with those he photographed he gave his loyalties to that community. And he would do just that for the rest of his life — defending the rights of the subjects of his photographs against unclear editing or careless editors or against the inevitable distortions embedded in a bureaucratic, corporate media structure. These loyalties took precedent over any other loyalties to the job, to the system, or to a sense of false nationalism. During World War II his rage was directed against censorship and his contempt was directed against those who did not extend themselves to meet the challenge of the great events around them. Later the focus changed, but the impulse never faltered.

By early 1944, Smith had amassed an impressive body of work and had used up or broken most of his equipment. He returned to the United States in March. Still feeling too far away from the actual combat he negotiated a new contract with *Life* magazine and returned to the South Pacific as a *Life* staff photographer in May. His first assignment, to cover the invasion of Saipan in June, 1944, provided him the access to ground combat that he had sought so long.

13

Saipan was fought around, among, and over the helpless and terrified civilians hiding in caves in the hills. When Smith finally reached the goal he had been aiming at for three years, he found himself in the midst of the pain and terror of innocent people caught up in frightening forces beyond their control. It was an acute situation, explosive and verging on the awesome. Smith wrote his impressions of this battle in an unpublished manuscript:

> ...very slowly the head of a dazed old man appeared. Then the rest began to follow, — but OH! how slowly, and how pitiable they were as they emerged from the smoke — weak, sick from the smoke, guts simply twisted from the fear they felt of us — and of their possible fate. Tiny babies on the backs of their mothers, older children, fathers, grandfathers — all human lumps of fright and terrible weariness — young and old so helpless.[8]

In this situation courage might consist of a grandfather cleaning a small child while surrounded by the armed figures of his possible death. Pain might sit in the curve of a soldier's back as he holds a mortally wounded baby. Grace might be seen in the face of a soldier helping an enemy to safety. The events are particular and very precise, real in their exact dimensions. With this experience, the rhetoric of patriotism was lost to Smith forever. His suspicions of large, loose, careless concepts were fixed and driven home for good.

> With sickness and realization that was sour in my throat, the scene pounded home to me but for the luck of U.S. birth my people could be these people, my children could be these children — DAMN THE MAKERS OF WARS!

> To most of these crushed people the United States was no more than a name — possibly a name to hate. And those that told them to hate (when they had not reason to hate) — those were the makers of wars. EVERY FILM THAT I EXPOSED WAS FROM MY HEART, IN THE BITTER CONDEMNATION OF WAR.[9]

If before he had wanted "...history to fall before my lens...," from this point on history would for him consist of individual people engaged in very specific acts in the midst of very precise events.

And it was within this existential situation on Saipan that Smith conclusively broke through that barrier of distance between himself and the subjects that he was photographing.

In a letter to his family, September 3, 1944, he wrote:

> ...a few of the pictures made on Saipan were close to being the best I have ever made. ...I do not believe I could have reached this close without my family. For these people of the pictures were my family — within possibility — and I saw my daughter, and my wife, and my mother, and my son, reflected in the tortured faces of another race. Accident of birth, accident of home — damn the rot of men that leads to wars. The bloody dying child I held momentarily in my arms while the life fluid seeped away and through my shirt and burned my heart into flaming hate — that child was my child....

And as he got physically closer to the heart of the action he broke through a psychological barrier as well. Human events take place within, and are surrounded by, a dome of emotionally charged space. We all recognize and instinctively respond to a myriad of spatial indicators each day. A certain distance or a certain stance places us outside of events as observers — another distance places us within events as participants. On Saipan, Smith learned to compose in a powerfully coherent way so as to put himself (and therefore the viewers sharing his stance) within the emotional sphere of the action. Smith would study and use the implications, variations, alterations, and possibilities of this discovery throughout the rest of his life.

After a scattered and unsuccessful attempt to cover the invasion of Guam, Smith "sets" his new perception in November with his photo story of the Army hospital in a cathedral on Leyte.

He wrote about the experience in a letter November 7, 1944:

> Have been in a hospital for the last three days . . . very carefully, very slowly, I worked and sweated and pulled a hospital story together that I feel may be one of my best stories of the war. . . .

This essay bristles with images made from within that specific emotional space. His stance, the placement of subjects within a circular composition, the handling of light, all work together to convey the sense of shared space in the photographs. Smith intuitively understood this development and he was satisfied with his work on Leyte.

Smith's early ambition to make a narrative history of the war had shifted focus by late 1944. He continued to mention a book, but by then it had a specific direction. It was anti-patriotic (but not anti-American) and anti-war (but not against this war).

Smith was embroiled in a complex, contradictory, highly-charged position. Fueled by his ambition and his guilt, focused by his rage and his beliefs, Smith continued to photograph in the heart of combat. His passionate intensity pushed him on through twelve campaigns in 1944 and 1945. Saipan, Guam, the Philippines, Leyte, the first Tokyo air raid, Iwo Jima, Okinawa — he continued to push himself beyond the limits of reason and then beyond the limits of luck. His friends, themselves experienced combat correspondents, became fearful for his safety. And on the thirteenth campaign, in the front lines of the battle for Okinawa, he was hit and severely wounded by shell fire.

Smith returned from World War II a wounded hero with the framework of a mature style. He had a powerful reputation, an unexcelled body of work and an awesome self-imposed commitment. He hoped that photography — his photography — could be used to better the human condition.

> I was after a set of pictures so that when people looked at them they would say, 'This is war' — that the people who were in the war would believe that I had truthfully captured what they had gone through . . . I worked in the framework that war is horrible. I want to carry on what I have tried to do in these pictures. War is a concentrated unit in the

world and these things are clearly and cleanly seen. Things like race prejudice, poverty, hatred and bigotry are sprawling things in civilian life, and not so easy to define as in war.[10]

Riding the wave of his fame during the years immediately following the war, Smith attempted to establish a public forum for his ideas about photography. For Smith this was a period of active group involvement and public statements. From July, 1946 to February, 1947 he was the president of the American Society of Magazine Photographers; his interests also brought him to the New York Photo League where he became its president in 1948. In his exhibitions, interviews, and writings he would continually argue for the moral uses of photojournalism and the responsibility of photographers and editors:

Photography is a potent medium of expression. Properly used it is a great power for betterment and understanding. Misused, it has and will fire much trouble. . . . The photographer must bear the responsibility for his work and its effect.[11]

I'm still searching desperately for the truth, for the answer to how to do a picture story. . . . The majority of photo stories require a certain amount of setting up, re-arranging and stage direction to bring pictorial and editorial coherency to the pictures. . . . If, however, the changes become a perversion of the actuality for the sole purpose of making a more dramatic or salable picture, the photographer has indulged in poetic license that shouldn't be. . . . I insist on doing it my way — just so long as that way is legitimate. . . . Photography is not just a job to me. I'm car-rying a torch with a camera, and it won't embarrass me if you say just that.[12]

World War II, its aftermath and the glum foregatherings of the Cold War had disrupted and destroyed the documentary approach to photography as a coherent, organized movement. But *Life* magazine and a few of the other mass magazines had survived the war and were in the strongest position they had ever enjoyed. Those magazines carried forward many of the humanist concerns inherited from the shattered documentary movement. Limited by their own structures and constricted by the developing pressures and fears of the Cold War, these magazines were nevertheless leading forces for the display of a humanistic ideology into the fifties. Smith had reluctantly continued to work for *Life* after the war and his work was helping form the shape and dimensions of that humanistic ideal in photojournalism. The warm, humane and democratic "Folk Singers" essay of 1947 was followed by "Trial by Jury" and then the pivotal "Country Doctor" in 1948.

In this essay Smith photographed the daily activities of a doctor in a small town in Colorado. Smith was sympathetic to this topic and he brought all of the lessons and broadened vocabulary that he had learned in the war to the making of this essay. Rather than attempting to dominate and structure the events of the doctor's life (a phenomenon of most previous photojournalism, which *Life* had become notorious for practicing), Smith "faded into the wallpaper."[13] First he spent time becoming acquainted with, and then becoming accepted as part of the doctor's community. Then, he quietly began to find the most powerful method of conveying the sense of that doctor's life.

Before the war Smith had depended upon

technical impressiveness or powerful composition to give his photography much of its emotional impact. During the war the rhetoric of the beautiful image had been controlled and made to serve the powerful subjects of each photograph. In "Country Doctor" Smith's strong compositional sense was again brought to the service of the narrative. He had established a new balance between the subject and its depiction — a balance that conveyed a sense of compassionate intimacy without sentiment or rhetoric. This new balance both within and among the images established a realistic sense of this doctor's character and of the situations where he displayed that character to the world. The essay offered a compellingly believable look into the life of a quiet man who had chosen to help relieve the pain of those around him.

The affirmative humanism and quietly powerful style of this story attracted immediate attention and praise and it soon came to define at least some of the possible future directions of the photo essay.

By the early fifties, the Cold War had destroyed the Photo League and with it most of Smith's fragile belief in the potential achievements of group efforts. But his desire to fight injustice with his own photography only intensified. Feeling embattled, guilty, and possibly threatened, he assumed even more personal responsibility and an even harsher, more suspicious attitude about institutions and organizations.

Smith moved into a situation filled with contradictions so intense that it verged on the schizophrenic. The weight of his arguments for a humanistic use of photography were fueled by the power of his *Life* essays and the prestige and authority that they brought to him. And yet Smith was balanced within a tense dance of oppositions at *Life*. Smith wanted to mine his art

out of the ore of commerce, his ambition was to transmit his profession into an art — moreover an art of the highest moral dimension. And *Life* magazine, honestly responding to the power (and battening on the prestige) of his work, boosted his creativity with one hand while attempting to structure and form its character to the limits of its own very real economic needs on the other. It was a marriage of necessity — both partners benefiting from the contract, both partners resentful and willing to abuse the relationship. Out of the irony inherent in this situation, a tension certainly fueled by Smith and possibly necessary to his creative spirit at the time, Smith would struggle to bring together some of the most significant photo essays in the history of the medium. Smith could produce mundane and even trivial work, but each year in the late forties and early fifties he would produce an essay that imbued that form with the possibility of expression and the potential for art. However, Smith was within an inherently unstable situation, ripe with rifts and clashes that ultimately would lead to a break-up.

Smith loved music and the theater. The two together make up the most frequent topic of his essays for *Life*. He brought his own dramatic sense to the theater and so was able to translate the typical staged tableaus of theatrical reportage photography into essays that were interesting and dramatic in their own right. And his passion for music is in his sympathetic portraits of musicians and composers — as in the portrait of the composer Charles Ives in 1949 or in the expressive "Recording Artists" made in 1951. With a wit, delicacy, compassion, and dedication that, in itself, matches that of the musicians which Smith was portraying, that essay conveys the many moods and tensions that occupy the feelings of dedicated artists embedded in the practice of their art. "Recording Artists" (1951) signals the full maturation of Smith's powers as a photo essayist. Its strengths have been overlooked simply because Smith published two other essays ("Spanish Village" and "Nurse Midwife"), of extraordinary power in the same year.

American theater in the 1950s used compression, elision and metaphor in plot, language and lighting to create a dramatic intensity that was designed to achieve a heightened sense of reality. Smith also believed in "... setting up, re-arranging and stage direction to bring pictorial and editorial coherency to pictures. ..." But he also believed that "If ... the changes become a perversion of the actuality ... that shouldn't be. ..."[14] He felt that this technique of altering for increasing dramatic emphasis or coherence should ultimately be used for the source of the "reality" of the subject. Thus he could establish an aesthetic that at one time argued for a rigorous honesty to the "spirit" of the subject, while it allowed him great flexibility in interpretation of that subject in his printing and presentation.

Music was vital to Smith. It sustained him. It was his "opiate against overnervousness,"[15] his continued source of inspiration and, apparently, his one untarnished connection with the creative act. He had wanted to write musical criticism after the war[16] and he would thereafter use the language of musical criticism to develop his personal vocabulary for a photographic aesthetic. He used such terms as "rhythm," "pacing," "crescendo" and "grace notes" to describe his own emotional patterns while photographing an event; to describe his conception of what constituted a good print; and to describe the characteristics of a well-organized group of photographs into a coherent photo essay. Smith would talk about "composing" an essay, using the term in the musical sense, as if he were composing a symphony.

Nineteen fifty-one was a good year for Smith. His volume of work was large and its quality was high. Two major essays published that year — "Spanish Village" and "Nurse Midwife" — shifted the ground of public understanding of the photo essay. Each of these essays had a mood and a texture of its own — each established its own authority — and so each in its own way helped to enlarge the possibilities of the essay as a medium of creative art.

"Spanish Village" has a narrative sweep that is both historic and humane. The protagonist in this essay is not any one individual; rather it is a way of life seen through the acts and faces of individuals that make up that culture. Through his powerfully expressive photographs, Smith presented a culture still in direct contact with its history, still tied to the seasonal rhythms of the land, still in harmony with the basic forces of the seasons of growth and harvest, the ceremonies of faith and social order, and the immutable facts of birth, labor and death.

The technocrats of Spain protested the essay's emphasis on the country's backwardness and poverty.[17] The people of the United States — wealthy, mobile, industrialized, dislocated and unfulfilled, and sliding into an era of uneasy confusion about the intimations of a loss of coherence in their lives — received Smith's essay in a wave of nostalgia and hope. His essay affirmed that the basic, powerful forces that they believed had shaped the destiny of mankind still existed. It touched and soothed a taut nerve vibrating in the hearts of many in this country. The essay caused a storm of response — a response that inexorably shifted Smith from journalist to artist in the public eye — and gave a heavy weight of conviction to the developing idea that photojournalism held the leading edge of creative photography during this era.

Maude Callen ("Nurse Midwife") was one of the persons Smith respected most of those that he met during a very full and active life. Maude was a black woman living in the Deep South of the early fifties. Maude had developed an enormous fund of courage, skill, talents, and intelligence in order to survive each day in the presence of the prejudice, bigotry, and hatred of the time. In the face of this daily pressure of psychological destruction, she had built a character strong enough not only to survive but also to provide an active force for comfort and assistance to those around her. Smith directed his essay to convey the strength, modesty, and courage of this exceptional woman.

"Spanish Village" was the portrait of a culture, "Nurse Midwife" was the portrait of a human being creating a life of value and meaning in the face of great difficulties. "Spanish Village" has a high percentage of distant views and establishing shots that relate the people with their structures and to their land; "Nurse Midwife" is shot almost exclusively from a middle distance or a close-up view; it contains a high percentage of interiors, and most of the exterior shots are carefully framed to convey a sense of close space. The photographs in this essay are filled with the clutter of the details, textures and surfaces of the objects that surrounded Maude's days. The composition is complexly and richly organized to bring this clutter into an order — an order that often has Maude as its center.

Smith wanted to use his photography to fight prejudice and hatred. This essay gave him an opportunity to do just that. His moving portrayal of Maude is a quietly affirmative view of the courage, strength, and dignity present in the human character.

By 1951, Smith had found his mature voice. His technique was superb. He was able to make individual photographs within each essay that were powerful and moving. He could modulate his style from essay to essay with an exceptional flexibility. He controlled all of the necessary elements of his art — the art of the photo essay — except one. He still was not able to control the exact presentation of his own work.

Every working photojournalist has faced the fact that many of his photographs — his good photographs — never reach publication. The depth of commitment in time and energy that Smith made to the subjects that he photographed was extensive and this commitment is reflected both in the quality and in the quantity of his images. It was not unusual for Smith to personally enlarge and mount several hundred photographs from each of his major essays for his own purposes. To cut an essay from, for example, 150 images to ten or fifteen or even thirty in order to meet the very real necessities of publishing must have been for Smith an exercise in exquisite agony. Each paring of images inevitably weakened the dense interlocking fabric of associations generated between the full body of images in the essay. For Smith the published essays could have remained little more than metaphors for the work of art that he saw and had constructed. Smith lived most of his life in a state of ironic frustration, knowing that his real work was not known.

This frustration would lead Smith within three years to a decision to quit *Life* and by so doing deprive himself of the strongest base of his power within the field. It was a complex and difficult decision, not easily made, but one that inexorably evolved out of his own evolution from journalist to artist.

But that decision was to come in the future

19

— in 1951 Smith was at a high point in his career. He had created a number of essays of major dimension that year and two of the essays would become, each in their own way, the benchmark of quality for the most humane and the most expressive potentials inherent in the photo essay as an art form. W. Eugene Smith, through the power of his photographs and the strength of his ideas, had helped to foster the evolution of his discipline from a trade into an art form and in that act had brought an increased sense of the possibilities of man and of the world to millions.

NOTES

1. The January 2, 1939 issue of *Life* had 182 photographs packed into 60 pages. The two issues of *Look* for May 1939 contained 380 photographs. *Newsweek* published 95 photos for the week of July 17, 1937. *Colliers* printed 5 color and 28 black and white photos during July, 1939. *Ken* published 104 photos in the March 23, 1939 issue. The January 1938 issue of *Now & Then* contained 172 photographs. The June 14, 1938 copy of *Pic* had 191 photographs. These references form an absolutely random and typical example of the flood of photographs being presented to the public view during this time.

2. The typical critical article of this time would usually discuss something of the photographer's accomplishments, his techniques, craftsmanship and "trade secrets" and then stop there. Both of the early articles about Smith — Roger Monsell, "News Photography's Prodigy," *Prize Photography* [*Everyday Photography*] 5 (Nov. 1940):12–13, 54–55 and Peter Martin, "The Kid Who Lives Photography," *Popular Photography* 13, (July 1943):19–22, 90–91 — also comment extensively about the passionate, dynamic, driving energy that was so much a part of Smith's character and working method. Such comment was unusual for the period.

3. Claim made by Smith's mother in an interview in: Herman G. Weinberg, "Mother Knows Best?" *Minicam Photography* 9 (Nov. 1945):62–65, 122, 124.

4. "Newspapers and Magazines," *1944 Britannica Book of the Year* (Chicago: Encyclopedia Britannica, 1944):501.

5. W. Eugene Smith, unpublished, untitled manuscript about his experiences aboard the U.S.S. Bunker Hill, 1943–1944. The W. Eugene Smith Archive, Center for Creative Photography, Tucson, Arizona. (The manuscript from the U.S.S. Bunker Hill is incomplete.)

6. Smith wrote an extensive series of letters to his family while he was in the South Pacific from 1943 to 1945. A portion of these letters have survived and are in the W. Eugene Smith Archive, Center for Creative Photography. Quoted materials not specifically noted are from this collection.

7. Smith, U.S.S. Bunker Hill manuscript: 136.

8. W. Eugene Smith, "The Struggle to Save," unpublished manuscript, p. 6, the W. Eugene Smith Archive, Center for Creative Photography. Manuscript is undated but written after April 1945 when Smith went to Saipan. Location among other Saipan written material and style of writing would presumably date the piece in 1945 or shortly after.

9. ibid.

10. Selma Robinson, "He Photographed the Real War," *P.M.'s Sunday Picture News*, magazine section, (26 May 1946):1, 7–15.

11. W. Eugene Smith, "Photographic Journalism," *Photo Notes* (June 1948):4–5.

12. James L. Collings, "Photography: Smith Carries Torch With His Camera," *Editor & Publisher*, (2 October 1948):46.

13. ibid.

14. ibid.

15. ibid.

16. Letter from Smith to John Hackett, Managing Editor of *Pageant* requesting a position as a music critic, 29 November 1945, W. Eugene Smith Archive, Center for Creative Photography.

17. Examples of this feeling are in: Gaspar Gomez de la Serna, "Carta al Editor de 'Life'," *Mundo Hispanico* (Madrid) 4th year (July 1951):17–19, and W. Fernandez Florez, "De la Leyenda Negra a la Foto Negra Sobre España," *Semana* (Madrid) 12th year (July 1951):15–17. These articles protested Smith's version of Spain as unfairly concentrating on rural poverty. Authors attempted to show that a more modern industrialized Spain existed.

GENE SMITH : A Personal Note

by John G. Morris

MIRACULOUSLY, the meaning of the life and work of W. Eugene Smith may at last become clear, now that he is gone.

An innate sense of his own destiny led Smith to collect and keep the evidence of his own genius: the thousands of prints over which he labored long and lonely in the dark, accompanied by Beethoven, Bach or Benny Goodman; the odds and ends of camera gear — two whole cartons just of lens hoods and lens caps; the scraps of paper on which he wrote diatribes against war, inhumanity, his own inadequacies and those of his editors; his 25,000 phonograph records, uncounted thousands of books, magazines, clippings, notes, letters — even his unpaid bills.

It is all — ten tons of it — being thoughtfully, even lovingly, preserved, at the University of Arizona's Center for Creative Photography in Tucson.

Will it answer the basic question: Who was this incredible man? Each of us who knew him searches memories for clues, the pieces of a puzzle.

My own begins with a day in New York in early September, 1939. World War II was perhaps five days old. At the outbreak of hostilities, within hours of Hitler's invasion of Poland, a British naval patrol had caught the German passenger liner Columbus in mid-Atlantic. Her crew scuttled her, to keep her out of the hands of the British, and after taking to life boats they had been picked up by passing freighters and brought into temporary internment at Ellis Island, in New York harbor.

Gene Smith, a 20-year-old freelance photographer working through Black Star picture agency, and I, a 22-year-old cub reporter, were assigned by *Life* magazine to cover the story. As we boarded the Ellis Island ferry at the Battery, I recall that we joked about our first "overseas" assignment of the war.

We were among the handful of Americans to look into the faces of some 450 uniformed Germans, in that first naval action that did not directly involve America. But the story was no big deal. It did not even make that week's *Life,* though it was later published in England.

That did not greatly matter, to Gene and to me. What did matter was that *Life* was providing us with tickets to our times. We had both begun working for *Life* in the fall of 1938, Gene as a freelance photographer hired at $25 a day, I as a "CBOB" (College Boy Office Boy) at $20 a week. Gene's first published picture, part of an essay on "Old Age" by several photographers, was of an old couple published in the Nov. 7, 1938 issue of *Life*. My early duties were to sort the mail, run copy for the printers to the Twentieth Century Limited, and get a daily carton of milk for the Publisher.

Life was already two years old. From the moment its first issue had appeared in November, 1936, a Bourke-White picture of the Fort Peck dam on its cover, the magazine had been a runaway success. In those days before television, it was *Life* that brought the picture into the living rooms of America.

For photographers the attraction of *Life* was irresistible. It was a handsome showcase — bringing instant attention from the entire photographic community. Whereas newspapers, wire services and ad agencies then buried the names of their photographers, *Life* cleverly exploited them. *Life* photographers became celebrity figures. "I'm from *Life*" was the only entrée one needed — to boudoir or board room, classroom or clubhouse, caucus or concert, humble homestead or luxury hotel.

So it was no great wonder that *Life* virtually had its choice of the world's most talented photographers. Many came as refugees from Nazi Europe: among them Robert Capa, Alfred Eisenstaedt, Hansel Mieth and her husband Otto Hagel. There was Dmitri Kessel, from the Ukraine via New York's fur district. There was Albanian-born Gjon Mili, who had developed stroboscopic lighting with Harold Edgerton, and Algerian-born John Phillips of the impeccable manners.

The Americans were equally diverse. Many were crack newspaper photographers, lured by better money and broader opportunity: Thomas D. McAvoy from the *Washington Daily News,* Frank Scherschel from the *Milwaukee Journal,* William Vandivert from the Hearst newspapers, George Strock from the *Los Angeles Times,* Bob Landry from the *Los Angeles Examiner,* Ed Clark from the *Nashville Tennessean.* Somewhat surprisingly, only one photographer, Carl Mydans, came from the great Farm Security Administration group of Roy Stryker.

Then there were the talented kids, who were just coming of shooting age as *Life* was born: Bernard Hoffman, a *Time* office boy from the Bronx, Eliot Elisofon from the lower East Side, Jerry Cooke and Ralph Morse of Pix who had assisted Eisenstaedt. There was the Fremont High School gang from Los Angeles: Mark Kauffmann, who had his first *Life* cover at 15, and his sidekicks John Dominis and Hank Walker. In San Francisco there was Peter Stackpole, whose daring photographs of the building of the Golden Gate bridge landed him a *Life* job in Hollywood. From Miami came David Douglas Duncan, who was soon to cover the war in the Pacific as a Marine.

Gene Smith was one of those kids. He had come to New York from Kansas by way of Notre Dame, in early 1937, age 18. He had gotten a starting job at *Newsweek* and been fired for insisting on using a "small" (2¼ x 2¼) format camera. He then made his way to Black Star, whose crowded but congenial offices in the Graybar building on Lexington Avenue resembled one huge filing cabinet.

Black Star had been founded in 1936 by three refugees from Berlin: Kurt Safranski, who had been a top editor of *Berliner Illustrierte Zeitung,* which could claim to be the continent's first real picture magazine; Ernst Mayer, who had run the German picture agency Mauritius; and Kurt Kornfeld, a former publisher of scientific books. The kindly Kornfeld was a father figure to the Black Star family, and Gene Smith was to name his first-born son Kurt Patrick Smith.

Black Star soon attracted a galaxy of stellar photographers, the nucleus being Europeans: Ralph Crane, Andreas Feininger, Fritz Goro, Philippe Halsman. But there were also Charles Steinheimer, a gangly kid from San Francisco, Kosti Ruohomaa, the sensitive son of a Maine blueberry farmer, and Ron Partridge, son of Imogen Cunningham.

Several Black Star photographers worked for *Life* virtually full-time at rates as low as $25 a day. The page rate was $50 and the photographer received whichever rate came out to his advantage. For example, if he shot a full-page picture in one afternoon he got $50; if he spent seven days shooting a five-page story he got $350. The freelance system worked well to *Life*'s advantage, saving the overhead of salaries, overtime and benefits.

Whereas most young photographers in those hungry late-depression days happily accepted *Life*'s conditions, Gene Smith was an exception. He rebelled against the system under which most *Life* photographers turned their film in to the lab for processing — in many cases to be edited by the lab chief, who would generally "over pick" to be on the safe side. Gene refused. He insisted on developing his own film and making his own prints — often assisted by his mother, who would also chauffeur him on jobs. He would not let the editors second-guess him by inspecting his "rejects." Consequently he forced himself to work around the clock, shooting by day, printing by night.

Life's editors thought that Smith took himself and his work too seriously, to the point of arrogance. There was often tension. In one instance in the spring of 1941, as one of the assistant picture editors, I had to take personal responsibility for choosing Gene from the roster of photographers for an assignment on the Ohio penitentiary. Nobody else wanted to handle him.

The editors, of course, had the final say as to which stories and pictures were used. Even Gene — at that point — did not presume to dictate that. *Life*'s hierarchy was then headed by Managing Editor John Shaw Billings, a tough-minded editor who had been transferred from *Time* just in time to save *Life* from chaos on the eve of its first issue. Billings declined to have anything to do with photographers. He had some reason. Photographers tend to love favorite pictures as mothers do their babies. Billings

wanted the freedom to make objective — and final — decisions. He refused to concern himself with how much time, money or heartbreak had gone into the making of a set of pictures. If it did not fit his formula for that week's issue it was discarded into the big "reject" basket in his office. And Gene Smith not only cared about his pictures; he also felt deeply about the people he photographed.

The duty of dealing with *Life*'s photographers fell to the crafty Wilson Hicks, one of *Life*'s two Executive Editors, a Missourian and former Features Editor of the Associated Press. His was a dubious privilege. He was the most likely scapegoat if things went wrong, the butt of denigrating jokes if things went right. *Life*'s photographers, a somewhat fickle lot, alternately feared him and fawned on him.

It was the job of Hicks and his assistants to weed the weekly batch of story suggestions, decide which should be covered, and match the photographer to the job. The generation of story ideas was the responsibility of *Life*'s other Executive Editor, Daniel Longwell, a Nebraskan and former Doubleday editor. He rode herd on the heads of *Life*'s departments, such as Newsfront, Science, Sports, Modern Living and Life Goes to a Party. Each was instructed to produce roughly three times as much material as the magazine could possibly publish. *Life*'s appetite for picture material was insatiable. Smith shot his share of the trivial: among the 159 pictures of his that *Life* published in 1941 were stories on "How to Salute," "Harlem's New Congeroo Gives Girls a Workout," and "On Sadie Hawkins Day, North Carolina Co-eds Show How to Kiss Girl-shy Boys." In the fashion of the day, many pictures were "set up," often with elaborate multi-flash systems.

Waste was built into the *Life* system; it was

thought that such internal competition was the only way to keep quality up. External competition was simply not recognized. *Look* and *Parade* closed on six-weeks' lead time as opposed to *Life*'s three days. *Life* was America's only true news picture magazine and, by its own boast, "America's most potent editorial force."

That force was being used by *Life* Editor-in-Chief Henry R. Luce and his colleagues to bring America into the war against Nazi Germany. But it was Imperial Japan that settled the issue of Intervention vs. Isolationism. The date was precise: December 7, 1941. It was also my 25th birthday.

I had been a pacifist in college, and a conscientious objector until Pearl Harbor. Gene was not. He had enthusiastically photographed many *Life* stories on the build-up of America's armed forces, had shot a series for *Collier's* on "Our Fighting Men," and for *Parade* had almost killed himself by triggering a staged "battle" scene (see Plate 12), using himself as model.

After Pearl Harbor Smith chafed for action, but he was not one of *Life*'s first chosen war correspondents — it was one of his periods of estrangement. After trying, and failing (for medical reasons), to get assigned to Edward Steichen's celebrated group of Navy combat photographers, he managed, in the fall of 1943, to get sent to the Pacific Theater as a War Correspondent for the Ziff-Davis magazines *Flying* and *Popular Photography*. After two months aboard cruisers he got assigned to the aircraft carrier Bunker Hill.

All wartime photo coverage was subject both to censorship and to "pooling." The big four of the picture "pool," automatically entitled to "front-row seats" with impending operations, were the three wire services and *Life*. Pictures taken by any one member of the pool were theoretically available to the other three members — as were pictures taken by other correspondents who were not even pool members.

Smith, representing only monthlies, and trade magazines at that, was frustrated in his efforts to cover vital, important action. Carrier war, in a sense, was cold war, whose distant targets provided no glimpse of a human enemy. One senses Smith's relief when he landed briefly on Tarawa, even though the bloody battle was over. In one incredible hour he intensely photographed the human carnage, of friend and foe. He would no longer look at war with the one-sided point of view of soldiers and most war correspondents. From Tarawa he would not turn back. He had accredited himself to humanity.

By the spring of 1944 it became clear to Smith's editors at Ziff-Davis that their arrangement with him did not make much sense. Under the pooling requirement, his best pictures were appearing in newspapers and *Life* long before they could be used in their slow-moving monthlies. Smith won his release from Ziff-Davis and joined the *Life* staff. He covered the battles for Saipan, for the Philippines, for Iwo Jima and for Okinawa, where he was almost killed in the process of taking his last war picture (see Plate 54). William Johnson has eloquently documented, in Gene's own words, the profound transformation that occurred in Smith in that tormented time.

I had lost personal touch with Gene late in 1943. I had gone off to war in the opposite direction, to the European Theater, as *Life*'s London Picture Editor. I was to edit the coverage and occasionally experience the war first-hand with such *Life* photographers as Robert Capa, Bob Landry, Ralph Morse, George Rodger, David Scherman, Frank Scherschel and George Silk.

It was Capa who taught me the most; my

classroom was the foxholes and hedgerows of Normandy and Brittany. Capa was a superb journalist — I've never known anyone with a sharper instinctive sense of a human situation. But Capa kept his cool. He hated to let himself get emotionally involved; perhaps because, early in the Spanish Civil War, he had lost the woman he loved under the treads of a tank.

Our war was different from Smith's. It was a war fought amidst the civilization of centuries against a foe whose language was at least familiar. But it was no less shattering. I recall the day a buzz-bomb landed near the London restaurant where I was having lunch. Going out to inspect the damage, I saw the wreckage of a jeep. Without thinking, I looked around for the driver, and there, in a bomb crater, I saw — his head.

I could not take that picture. I censored it in my heart. But often I thought of it, and wondered if we, on *Life* and in the press, were really telling the story that needed to be told. Gene Smith obviously had similar concerns. When, two years later, I saw his "War" exhibition at the Camera Club in New York, his pictures hit me with the shock of revelation. In that one room I saw at last what I so deeply felt but could not express. It helped prepare me to confront the wars that were to come.

Gene Smith did not go on to those wars. He found other battles — in his own words against "race prejudice, poverty, hatred and bigotry," and found them "not so easy to define as ... war." The maturity of viewpoint and brilliance of style he achieved in war were rewarded with a photographic intensity that, in my judgment, no photographer living or dead has surpassed.

But it seemed, for many months after World War II, that Gene Smith might never take another picture. A day of grim determination came in the summer of 1946: "Two painful, helpless years (had) followed my multiple wounding, during which time I had to stifle my restless spirit into a state of impassive, non-creative suspension, while the doctors by their many operations slowly tried to repair me. . . . But now, this day, I would endeavor to refute two years of negation. On this day, for the first time since my injuries, I would try to make the camera work for me, would try to force my body to control the mechanics of the camera; and, as well, I would try to command my creative spirit out of its exile."

The result was "The Walk to Paradise Garden," of his children Patrick and Juanita walking hand in hand into the woods. At first a

W. Eugene Smith: The Walk to Paradise Garden, 1946.

private picture, unpublished for years, it became famous after Edward Steichen chose it to conclude "The Family of Man." It is now one of the celebrated images of the century.

Returning to the *Life* staff, Gene resolved not to go forward by going backward — to the kind of transient and trivial assignments that had characterized the prewar years. He sought to establish himself on high new ground. A hint of it came with "Folk Singers," a delightful, nostalgic story on mountain music that appeared in October, 1947. But the big breakthrough came with "Country Doctor" in September, 1948, the story of a physician in a small Colorado town from which Gene refused to return until he had satisfied *his own* requirements, not just those of *Life*'s editors. They were more easily satisfied.

As Picture Editor of the *Ladies' Home Journal* at the time, I recall being elated for Gene, and envious at the same time. We were doing a fine documentary series in the same genre called "How America Lives," using some of the photographers who had been trained by Roy Stryker in Farm Security Administration days and by Edward Steichen in wartime. But the *Journal* would never give more than eight pages to such a story, and the layouts had to accommodate a lot of text. At *Life*, "Country Doctor" took over eleven pages, and the writing hardly got in the way at all.

I had left *Life* in 1946, a rebel more against the personnel system that pitted man against man than against the content of the magazine. Gene continued to be an inspiration. Together we fought on the home front of the Cold War, the McCarthy front. He took the leadership of the Photo League, an organization blacklisted by the Attorney General, in order to rally round the cause of freedom of thought and association. I spoke at the League and spent free time in battling along with other writers and artists against the blacklisters.

In one incredible burst of energy, Gene published in *Life,* in the year 1951, in addition to five theater stories, the essay "Recording Artists," a gallery of sensitive working portraits of a score of great performers; "Spanish Village,"

most famous of all *Life*'s photo essays; and "Nurse Midwife," Smith's own favorite essay, on "the greatest human being I have ever known."

As he demanded more and more of himself, Smith also demanded more and more from his editors. They failed to meet his challenge — on his extraordinary terms. A more skillful politician might have been more persuasive; he was abrasive. In 1952 there was only one *Life* essay, "Chaplin at Work." Now he was often separated from his family, drank heavily — although he never seemed to get drunk — and went through prolonged periods of despair alleviated only by his own brand of black humor.

Looking back on that time, Smith told Jim Hughes for *Quest/77:* "It is ironic that I reached the greatest heights of my powers during the most destructive time of my life. From 1950 on, everything I touched, wrote, thought about became more wildly free, disciplined, and envisioned. It kept on growing into the early '60s, when it began to decline in malnutrition, poverty, and blackballing."

Gene Smith died, so far as *Life* was concerned, when he resigned, age 36, in 1954. They would publish him again, but he was no longer part of *Life*'s creative process. And *Life* itself would die, age 36, in 1972.

But Gene was far from through: ahead lay his monumental work on Pittsburgh; a powerful small essay on mental health in Haiti; a searing exposé of chemical pollution in Minamata, Japan, done with his second wife Aileen; and a host of other works. Despite poverty and ill health he continued to print prodigiously, leaving more than ten thousand "master prints" and uncounted work prints behind at the time of his death in Tucson in 1978.

Now, the Center for Creative Photography will have his great work for future generations.

A SELECTION
OF PHOTOGRAPHS
BY W. EUGENE SMITH

The Years 1938-1951

EARLY WORK (1938–1943)

Plate 1

Plate 2

Plate 3

Plate 4

Plate 5

Plate 6

Plate 7

Plate 8

Plate 9

Plate 10

Plate 11

Plate 12

WORLD WAR II: U.S.S. BUNKER HILL (1943–1944)

Plate 13

Plate 14

Plate 15

Plate 16

Plate 17

WORLD WAR II: AIR STRIKES, MARSHALL ISLANDS (1944)

Plate 18

Plate 19

Plate 20

Plate 21

Plate 22

WORLD WAR II:
SAIPAN (1944)

Plate 23

Plate 24

Plate 25

Plate 26

Plate 27

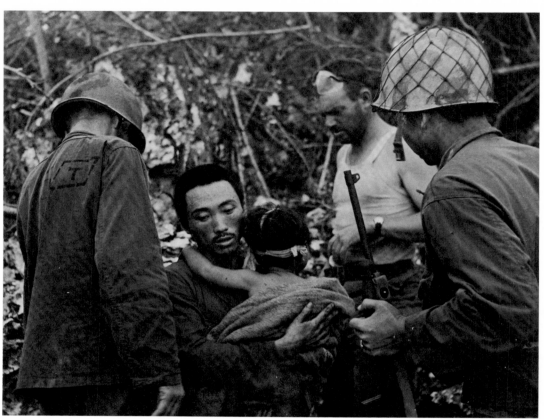

Plate 28

Plate 29

Plate 30

WORLD WAR II: HOSPITAL ON LEYTE (1944)

Plate 31

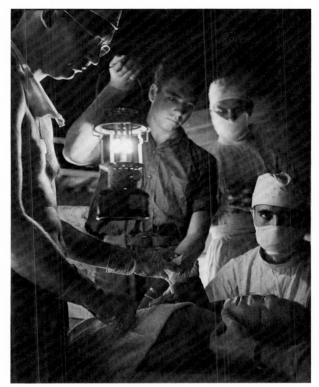

Plate 32

Plate 33

WORLD WAR II: IWO JIMA (1945)

Plate 34

Plate 35

Plate 36

Plate 37

WORLD WAR II:
OKINAWA (1945)

Plate 38

Plate 39

Plate 40

Plate 41

Plate 42

Plate 43

Plate 44

Plate 45

Plate 46

Plate 47

WORLD WAR II:
OKINAWA (1945)

"24 HOURS WITH
INFANTRYMAN
TERRY MOORE"

Plate 48

Plate 49

Plate 50

Plate 51

Plate 52

Plate 53

Plate 54

W. Eugene Smith's final photograph of
World War II, of the mortar burst that
wounded him, on Okinawa, 3:30 p.m.,
May 22, 1945.

FOLK SINGERS (1947)

Plate 55

Plate 56

NEW MEXICO
(1947)

Plate 57

Plate 58

COUNTRY DOCTOR (1948)

Plate 59

Plate 60

Plate 61

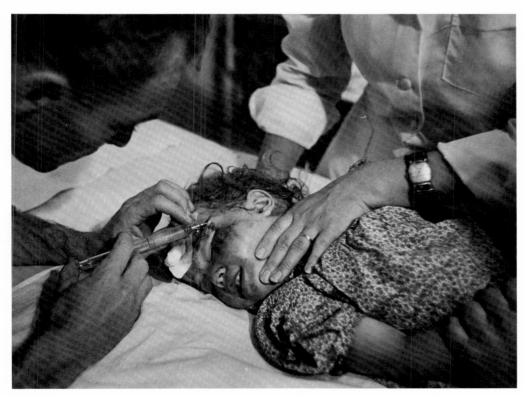

Plate 62

HARD TIMES
ON BROADWAY (1949)

Plate 63

Plate 64

Plate 65

DEATH OF A SALESMAN (1949)

Plate 66

COMPOSER
CHARLES IVES
(1949)

Plate 67

THEATRE GIRL
(1949)

Plate 68

LIFE WITHOUT GERMS (1949)

Plate 69

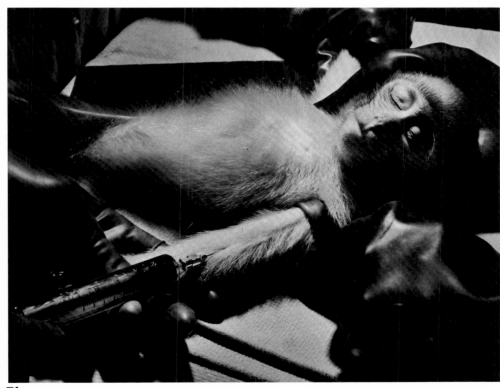

Plate 70

TAFT AND OHIO
(1949)

Plate 71

Plate 72

Plate 73

Plate 74

GREAT BRITAIN, WALES (1950)

Plate 75

Plate 76

Plate 77

Plate 78

RECORDING ARTISTS
(1951)

Plate 79

Plate 80

Plate 81

Plate 82

SPANISH VILLAGE (1951)

Plate 83

Plate 84

Plate 85

Plate 86

Plate 87

Plate 88

Plate 89

A PLAY FOR CHURCHES (1951)

Plate 90

Plate 91

Plate 92

NURSE MIDWIFE (1951)

Plate 93

Plate 94

Plate 95

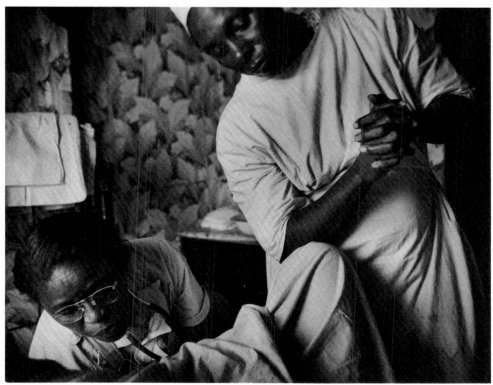

Plate 96

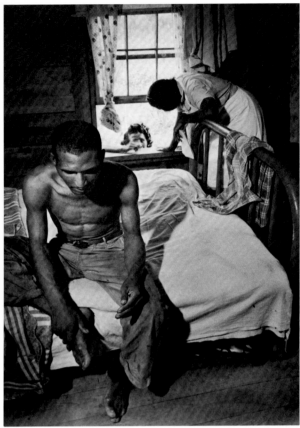

Plate 97

Plate 98

Plate 99

List of Plates

Titles in quotation marks appear in Smith's handwriting on the mount or verso of the photograph; other titles are descriptive.

1. "Untitled, no. 20," 1941.
   34.0 x 26.3 cm.

2. Betty Hutton in *Miss Muffet,* 1940.
   Published in *Life,* March 11, 1940, p. 51.
   33.8 x 26.2 cm.

3. "Irene Castle and Alex Fisher," 1939.
   Published in *Life,* August 21, 1939, p. 19.
   33.7 x 25.7 cm.

4. Robert 'Red' Rolfe, 1940.
   Published in *Colliers,* August 17, 1940, p. 13.
   31.1 x 24.5 cm.

5. "Second," 1942.
   Boxing assistant Ray Arcel.
   Published in *American Magazine,*
       May, 1942, p. 82.
   33.8 x 26.8 cm.

6. Carl Sandburg Listening to Marianne Lorrain
       Reciting His Poetry, 1941.
   Published in *Colliers,* June 14, 1941, p. 22.
   33.4 x 25.9 cm.

7. Construction, ca. 1942.
   33.7 x 26.0 cm.

8. "Stranger in Town," 1942.
   Published in *Parade,* November 29, 1942, p. 2.
   29.4 x 24.6 cm.

9. "Gas Attack," 1938.
   Published in *Life,* December 19, 1938, p. 57.
   33.5 x 25.9 cm.

10. American Commandos, 1942.
    Published in *Parade,* July 5, 1942, p. 2.
    26.6 x 32.6 cm.

11. "Off the Assembly Line," ca. 1943.
    30.3 x 26.4 cm.

12. Self Portrait, 1942.
    Published in *Parade,* September 13, 1942, p. 5.
    31.4 x 26.3 cm.

13. " 'Avenger' in Landing Circle Over U.S.S. Bunker
    Hill," ca. December, 1943.
    26.6 x 34.0 cm.

14. "Wheeling 2,000-pound Bomb on the U.S.S.
    Bunker Hill," ca. November, 1943.
    From the essay "A Carrier at Work," *Flying,*
    May, 1944.
    27.5 x 26.5 cm.

15. "Loading a 'Helldiver' with 50-caliber Shells,"
    ca. November, 1943.
    From the essay "A Carrier at Work," *Flying,*
    May, 1944.
    28.8 x 26.4 cm.

16. "On the Way to a Strike, from the U.S.S. Bunker
    Hill," ca. January, 1944.
    26.7 x 31.8 cm.

17. "A Memorial Service on the Carrier Deck,
    U.S.S. Bunker Hill," February, 1944.
    26.0 x 33.5 cm.

18. Ships Burning off Truk Island, February, 1944.
    10.9 x 32.8 cm.

19. Japanese Attack on U.S.S. Bunker Hill during
    Rabaul Raid, November, 1943.
    29.6 x 26.4 cm.

20. 'Avengers' over Tinian Island, February, 1944.
    Published in "Navy Attacks the Islands," *Life,*
    May 8, 1944, pp. 22–23.
    32.9 x 27.0 cm.

21. " 'Avengers' above Engebi Island," January, 1944.
    Published in *Flying,* July, 1944.
    34.3 x 26.9 cm.

22. "Bomb Splattered Air Strip (Engebi),"
    January, 1944.
    26.6 x 33.9 cm.

23. Unknown Marine, Saipan, June, 1944.
    From the essay "Saipan," *Life,* August 28, 1944.
    34.0 x 26.5 cm.

24. "Saipan Marines Watching for Jap Snipers Who
    are on Distant Hills in Bushes," June, 1944.
    From the essay "Saipan," *Life,* August 28, 1944.
    26.5 x 29.7 cm.

25. Civilians Caught in War, Saipan, June, 1944.
    From the essay "Saipan," *Life,* August 28, 1944.
    31.8 x 25.4 cm.

26. Saipan, June, 1944.
    From the essay "Saipan," *Life,* August 28, 1944.
    33.6 x 26.3 cm.

27. Saipan, June, 1944.
    From the essay "Saipan," *Life,* August 28, 1944.
    26.7 x 33.9 cm.

28. Saipan, June, 1944.
    From the essay "Saipan," *Life,* August 28, 1944.
    26.7 x 34.0 cm.

29. "Working under Fire, Saipan," June, 1944.
    From the essay "Saipan," *Life,* August 28, 1944.
    26.9 x 31.5 cm.

30. "American Dead (1,000) when Japs Broke
    through on Saipan," June, 1944.
    From the essay "Saipan," *Life,* August 28, 1944.
    26.6 x 33.7 cm.

31. Hospital on Leyte, 1944.
    From the essay "Hospital on Leyte," *Life,*
    December 25, 1944.
    32.0 x 35.2 cm.

32. Operation, Leyte, October–November, 1944.
    From the essay "Hospital on Leyte," *Life,*
    December 25, 1944.
    33.9 x 26.5 cm.

33. "Priest — Lew Ayres — Patient, Leyte,"
    October–November, 1944.
    From the essay "Hospital on Leyte,"
    December 25, 1944.
    26.7 x 33.8 cm.

34. Iwo Jima, D-Day, February, 1945.
    From the essay "Marines Win Bloody, Barren
    Sands of Iwo," *Life,* March 12, 1945.
    22.8 x 33.8 cm.

35. Iwo Jima, D-Day, February, 1945.
    From the essay "Marines Win Bloody, Barren
    Sands of Iwo," *Life,* March 12, 1945.
    26.7 x 34.0 cm.

36. Iwo Jima, February, 1945.
    From the essay "The Battlefield of Iwo," *Life,*
    April 9, 1945.
    25.0 x 34.0 cm.

37. Iwo Jima, February, 1945.
    From the essay "The Battlefield of Iwo," *Life,*
    April 9, 1945.
    27.7 x 26.4 cm.

38. Flares, Okinawa, April, 1945.
    30.9 x 26.8 cm.

39. Tanks, Men, Okinawa, April, 1945.
    26.5 x 34.0 cm.

40. Okinawa (The Crag), April, 1945.
    23.6 x 34.0 cm.

41. Okinawa, April, 1945.
    23.1 x 34.0 cm.

42. "Burning the Crag on Okinawa," May, 1945.
    Published in *Life,* May 14, 1945, p. 96.
    34.0 x 26.5 cm.

43. Okinawa, April, 1945.
    21.2 x 27.7 cm.

44. Okinawa, May, 1945.
    25.0 x 33.4 cm.

45. "Front Line on Okinawa," April, 1945;
    "One Rifleman's First Day of Combat;
    No Speeches, No Flags, No Glory."
    33.9 x 26.6 cm.

46. "Front Line Okinawa," April, 1945.
    24.4 x 33.7 cm.

47. "Whole Patrol Wiped Out, Okinawa,"
    April, 1945.
    25.8 x 33.8 cm.

48. Terry Moore, May, 1945.
    From the essay "Americans Battle for Okinawa:
    24 Hours with Infantryman Terry Moore,"
    Life, June 18, 1945.
    34.2 x 26.6 cm.

49. "From 24 Hours with Infantryman, (22nd) 7th
    Division," May, 1945.
    From the essay "Americans Battle for Okinawa:
    24 Hours with Infantryman Terry Moore,"
    Life, June 18, 1945.
    34.5 x 26.9 cm.

50. Terry Moore, May, 1945.
    From the essay "Americans Battle for Okinawa:
    24 Hours with Infantryman Terry Moore,"
    Life, June 18, 1945.
    34.2 x 26.4 cm.

51. Terry Moore, May, 1945.
From the essay "Americans Battle for Okinawa:
24 Hours with Infantryman Terry Moore,"
Life, June 18, 1945.
21.0 x 26.3 cm.

52. Terry Moore, May, 1945.
From the essay "Americans Battle for Okinawa:
24 Hours with Infantryman Terry Moore,"
Life, June 18, 1945.
26.7 x 34.3 cm.

53. Terry Moore, May, 1945.
From the essay "Americans Battle for Okinawa:
24 Hours with Infantryman Terry Moore,"
Life, June 18, 1945.
30.0 x 26.4 cm.

54. (untitled), 1945.
(This is the last photograph Smith made of
World War II, Okinawa, 3:30 p.m.,
May 22, 1945.)
5.5 x 5.5 cm.

55. Uncle Joe Orr, 1947.
From the essay, "Folk Singers," *Life,*
October 20, 1947.
30.6 x 26.7 cm.

56. Sarah Bailey and Fiddlin' Bill Hensley at
Asheville, N.C. Folk Festival, 1947.
From the essay, "Folk Singers," *Life,*
October 20, 1947.
21.8 x 34.0 cm.

57. New Mexico, 1947.
From an unpublished essay.
31.2 x 26.6 cm.

58. New Mexico, 1947.
From an unpublished essay.
32.5 x 26.8 cm.

59. Dr. Ceriani Making a House Call
in the Rain, 1948.
From the essay, "Country Doctor," *Life,*
September 20, 1948.
34.0 x 26.6 cm.

60. Dr. Ceriani Carrying Injured Boy
to Hospital, 1948.
From the essay, "Country Doctor," *Life,*
September 20, 1948.
26.8 x 34.3 cm.

61. Dr. Ceriani Administering to
Lee Marie Wheatly, 1948.
From the essay, "Country Doctor," *Life,*
September 20, 1948.
26.6 x 34.4 cm.

62. Dr. Ceriani Administering to
Lee Marie Wheatly, 1948.
From the essay, "Country Doctor," *Life,*
September 20, 1948.
26.0 x 34.0 cm.

63. (untitled), 1949.
From the essay, "Hard Times on Broadway,"
Life, February 14, 1949.
34.2 x 26.7 cm.

64. (untitled), 1949.
From the essay, "Hard Times on Broadway,"
Life, February 14, 1949.
34.1 x 21.8 cm.

65. (untitled), 1949.
From the essay, "Hard Times on Broadway,"
Life, February 14, 1949.
26.2 x 34.1 cm.

66. Lee J. Cobb as Willy Loman in Arthur Miller's
Death of a Salesman, 1949.
From the essay, "Death of a Salesman," *Life,*
February 21, 1949.
34.1 x 26.4 cm.

67. Charles Ives, 1949.
From the article, "Composer Charles Ives," *Life,*
October 31, 1949.
30.5 x 23.7 cm.

68. Jean Pearson, 1949.
From the essay, "Theatre Girl," *Life,*
November 21, 1949.
26.7 x 33.9 cm.

69. Rabbit in Germproof Chamber, Notre Dame's
Laboratory of Bacteriology, 1949.
From the essay "Life Without Germs," *Life,*
September 26, 1949.
27.0 x 33.6 cm.

70. Blood Sample from Germless Monkey, Notre
Dame's Laboratory of Bacteriology, 1949.
From the essay, "Life Without Germs," *Life,*
September 26, 1949.
26.6 x 34.2 cm.

71. Youngstown, Ohio Steel Mill, 1949.
    From the essay, "Taft and Ohio," *Life,*
    November 28, 1949.
    33.3 x 26.3 cm.

72. Rail Worker Joseph Hunter, 1949.
    From the essay, "Taft and Ohio," *Life,*
    November 28, 1949.
    26.3 x 32.0 cm.

73. Refinery Man, Sohio Plant, Cleveland, Ohio, 1949.
    From the essay, "Taft and Ohio," *Life,*
    November 28, 1949.
    33.3 x 25.8 cm.

74. Howard Taft, 7:30 a.m., Sidney Hotel,
    Sidney, Ohio, 1949.
    From the essay, "Taft and Ohio," *Life,*
    November 28, 1949.
    26.9 x 34.2 cm.

75. (untitled), 1950.
    From the essay, "Britain's Future is Put Up to
    Voters," *Life,* February 20, 1950.
    26.3 x 34.0 cm.

76. (untitled), 1950.
    From the essay, "Britain's Future is Put Up to
    Voters," *Life,* February 20, 1950.
    26.8 x 31.7 cm.

77. (untitled), 1950.
    From the essay, "Britain's Future is Put Up to
    Voters," *Life,* February 20, 1950.
    23.2 x 34.2 cm.

78. (untitled), 1950.
    From the essay, "Britain's Future is Put Up to
    Voters," *Life,* February 20, 1950.
    23.4 x 34.2 cm.

79. Wanda Landowska, 1951.
    From the essay, "Recording Artists," *Life,*
    March 26, 1951.
    33.5 x 23.4 cm.

80. (untitled), 1951.
    From the essay, "Recording Artists," *Life,*
    March 26, 1951.
    26.3 x 34.0 cm.

81. Gregor Piatigorsky, 1951.
    From the essay, "Recording Artists," *Life,*
    March 26, 1951.
    26.7 x 33.9 cm.

82. Conductor Guido Cantelli, 1951.
    From the essay, "Recording Artists," *Life,*
    March 26, 1951.
    27.0 x 34.0 cm.

83. (untitled), 1950.
    From the essay, "Spanish Village," *Life,*
    April 9, 1951.
    33.9 x 26.6 cm.

84. (untitled), 1950.
    From the essay, "Spanish Village," *Life,*
    April 9, 1951.
    31.9 x 26.7 cm.

85. (untitled), 1950.
    From the essay, "Spanish Village," *Life,*
    April 9, 1951.
    26.6 x 34.0 cm.

86. (untitled), 1950.
    From the essay, "Spanish Village," *Life,*
    April 9, 1951.
    24.2 x 34.0 cm.

87. (untitled), 1950.
    From the essay, "Spanish Village," *Life,*
    April 9, 1951.
    23.7 x 33.9 cm.

88. (untitled), 1950.
    From the essay, "Spanish Village," *Life,*
    April 9, 1951.
    33.6 x 23.5 cm.

89. (untitled), 1950.
    From the essay, "Spanish Village," *Life,*
    April 9, 1951.
    25.5 x 34.3 cm.

90. Abraham (Pvt. King) Contemplates Sacrificing
    his Son Issac (Pvt. Able), 1951.
    From the essay, "A Play for Churches," *Life,*
    November 12, 1951.
    34.0 x 26.6 cm.

91. Job (Cpt. Joe Adams) Brings Body of Absalom
    (Pvt. Able), 1951.
    From the essay, "A Play for Churches," *Life,*
    November 12, 1951.
    25.9 x 34.1 cm.

92. Hearing the Voice of God (Cpt. Adams), 1951.
    From the essay, "A Play for Churches," *Life,*
    November 12, 1951.
    24.0 x 33.3 cm.

93. (untitled), 1951.
From the essay, "Nurse Midwife," *Life,*
December 3, 1951.
26.5 x 34.0 cm.

94. (untitled), 1951.
From the essay, "Nurse Midwife," *Life,*
December 3, 1951.
26.5 x 33.8 cm.

95. (untitled), 1951.
From the essay, "Nurse Midwife," *Life,*
December 3, 1951.
26.7 x 34.2 cm.

96. (untitled), 1951.
From the essay, "Nurse Midwife," *Life,*
December 3, 1951.
27.0 x 34.0 cm.

97. (untitled), 1951.
From the essay, "Nurse Midwife," *Life,*
December 3, 1951.
33.4 x 22.8 cm.

98. (untitled), 1951.
From the essay, "Nurse Midwife," *Life,*
December 3, 1951.
34.0 x 26.7 cm.

99. (untitled), 1951.
From the essay, "Nurse Midwife," *Life,*
December 3, 1951.
26.1 x 33.5 cm.

THE W. EUGENE SMITH ARCHIVE

WHEN W. EUGENE SMITH moved to Tucson, Arizona to teach at the University of Arizona, the freight manifest for his possessions was listed at 44,000 pounds. At the time of his death on October 15, 1978 the Center for Creative Photography took on the responsibility of organizing and distributing the enormous quantity of materials that he had accumulated during his lifetime. His cameras, darkroom equipment, tools and furniture were distributed to his heirs and to others. His negatives, contact sheets, proof and study prints, book dummies and magazine layouts, his tearsheets, letters and manuscripts, personal and business files and memorabilia came to the W. Eugene Smith Archive at the Center for Creative Photography. The Center also obtained his large personal collection of books and magazines, phonograph records and audiotapes. The Center also located, organized, identified and eventually acquired over 2,600 photographs of the more than 9,000 photographic prints that were in the Smith Estate. W. Eugene Smith's previous lifestyle, coupled with his move to Arizona and sudden tragic illness and death had left this large mass of materials in a state of chaos. At the time of publication of this volume the scores of thousands of items in the Archive are still not completely organized and processed for public use. However, the core of the collection, over 3,000 individual images that Smith culled from his thousands of negatives, enlarged and often mounted, have been sorted, at least tentatively identified and added to the collections. This issue of the *Center for Creative Photography* is designed to bring some of the wealth of the Archive to a broader public.

WILLIAM JOHNSON
Curator
W. Eugene Smith Archive

St. Nicholas Arena, N.Y., 1954.
79:045:007

N.Y.C., 1948.
79:045:001

Detroit, 1954.
79:045:006

Acquisitions Highlight: Robert Frank

THE SWISS-BORN PHOTOGRAPHER Robert Frank, who had been successfully free-lancing in the United States since 1947, received a Guggenheim Grant in 1955 to photograph America. The results of his cross-country automobile trek were at first refused for publication because the imagery was considered controversial. Frank's vision of America included desolate highway landscapes, small "roadside events," "cool" teenagers and others on the fringes of society. These pictures were often composed without regard for traditional landscape and portrait schemes. In 1959 the avant-garde firm Grove Press published the Guggenheim work in this country as *The Americans*. A defiant, poetic statement by author Jack Kerouac introduced the pictures.

When seven editors of *Popular Photography* expanded the usually unimposing book review column in the May 1960 issue to comment on Frank's book, their reactions to it were defensive and disparaging. While the editors acknowledged Frank's expert use of the new "available light" camera technology, they were appalled by the bitterness they felt his pictures displayed. Criticism of the book as "idiosyncratic," "an attack on America," "without love," and even "tongue-in-cheek," reflect the editors' ambivalence towards Frank's subject matter and technique. Several writers attributed the disheartening mood to an extreme style of photographing, while others felt that a narrow or spiteful selection of subjects was responsible for "the immense gray tragic boredom" within the pictures.

Most critics of the period were unable to see that Frank was generating a new, significant subject matter from America's mundane sites and ignored citizens. Nor were critics able to predict that Frank's style would vitalize the next generation of small-camera photographers. Frank's own reconsideration of the Guggenheim period work, *The Lines of My Hand,* was published in 1972. This revealing and tender reassessment of his family, career and artistic associates includes additional work that balances Frank's, and the viewer's, response to the American scene of the 1950s.

If it is true that the picturing of an event gives the event credibility, then Frank's photographs of previously "invisible" particles of American culture have had a measurable effect on the culture itself. These photographs make us value unremarkable places and ask us to reconsider "unacceptable" forms of behavior. Frank's work is not irreverent. Rather, it offers a broadened resource for significance and choice in a potentially alienating world.

SUSAN E. COHEN

Ms. Cohen is a doctoral candidate in Art History at Boston University and Boston University Rockefeller Foundation Fellow for 1980/81. She has done extensive research at the Center for Creative Photography in the subject of American landscape photography.

The Center has recently acquired ten photographs by Robert Frank: two from *The Americans,* five from *The Lines of My Hand,* and three others. Nine of these prints are the gift of Mr. and Mrs. Harry H. Lunn, Jr., and the tenth print was purchased, bringing the Center's collection of Frank prints to twenty.

Acquisitions

JANUARY THROUGH JUNE 1979

THE FOLLOWING LIST is a name index to research material — primarily photographs and correspondence — acquired by the Center during the first half of 1979. Space has prohibited the itemization of very large collections and has limited the documentation of medium-sized collections of 10 to 30 photographs. (An exception has been made in this listing for the Robert Heinecken entry because of the unique nature of each of the works listed.) We will be pleased to provide a fuller description of anything in this listing. The acquisition of photographs by Robert Frank is discussed more fully in the Acquisitions Highlight section.

A number of the acquisitions during this period were made possible through a grant from the National Endowment for the Arts under the Museum Purchase Plan. This grant was matched by awards from the Polaroid Foundation, Valley National Bank (of Arizona), First National Bank of Arizona, and the Arizona Bank. Purchases made from this fund are designated Special Purchase in this listing.

Compiled by Jan Stevenson and Sherrie Denton, Curatorial Assistants.

ADAMS, ANSEL

Ten mural sized gelatin silver prints.
"Aspens, New Mexico," 1958.
76:562:006

"Board and Thistles, San Francisco, California,"
1932.
76:562:001

"Grand Tetons and Snake River, Wyoming," n.d.
76:562:002

"Leaves, Mt. Rainier National Park," n.d.
79:021:003

"Merced River, Cliffs of Cathedral Rock, Autumn,"
1939.
76:562:004

"Oak Tree and Cliffs of Cathedral Rocks," n.d.
76:562:005

"Pine Branches and Lichens, Yosemite National
Park, California," 1962.
76:562:003

"Sequoia Gigantea Roots, Yosemite National Park,"
n.d.
79:021:004

"Stream, Sea, Clouds, Rodeo Lagoon," n.d.
79:021:002

"Tar Paper and Nails," n.d.
79:021:001

Collection of Ansel Adams.
Twelve photographs by other photographers:
Roger Camp; Neil Chapman; J. L. Day;
George Fry, III; Kevin Hass; Chuck Henningsen;
R. F. McGraw; Alan Ross, G.O.S.;
George Upham. (Spelling of Upham not
legible on print.)
Processes and sizes vary.
Gift of Ansel and Virginia Adams.
79:015:001–012

Installation photographs, checklists and research
material relating to the exhibition, *Photographs
1923–1963, The Eloquent Light,* directed by
Nancy Newhall, 1963, and subsequent traveling
exhibitions directed by Beaumont Newhall.
Gift of Beaumont Newhall.

Barron, Susan. See: STRAND, PAUL.
Portraits of Paul Strand.

BERGER, PAUL

"2418 A," 1978.
Gelatin silver print. 30.5 x 16.3 cm.
Purchase.
79:034:003

"Camera Text or Picture #1," 1979.
Gelatin silver print. 28.0 x 41.7 cm.
Purchase.
79:034:001

"Camera Text or Picture #2," 1979.
Gelatin silver print. 28.0 x 41.7 cm.
Purchase.
79:034:002

BLOCH, ERNEST

Papers.
Photocopies of musical programs, scores and
    sketches.
Gift of Suzanne Bloch.

BOUGHTON, ALICE

"G. K. Chesterton," n.d.
Platinum print. 20.6 x 14.8 cm.
Purchase.
79:019:005

Untitled, n.d. (Portrait of J. Forbes Robertson.)
Platinum print. 18.9 x 13.4 cm.
Purchase.
79:019:001

Untitled, n.d. (Portrait of Paul Orlenff.)
Platinum print. 20.9 x 16.0 cm.
Purchase.
79:019:002

Untitled, n.d. (Woman holding plate of fruit.)
Platinum print. 18.3 x 6.5 cm.
Purchase.
79:019:003

Untitled, n.d. (Young woman holding a flower.)
Platinum print. 20.8 x 15.8 cm.
Purchase.
79:019:004

Untitled, ca. 1920–25. (Portrait of Alia Mazimova.)
Platinum print. 19.0 x 13.6 cm.
Purchase.
79:019:006

BRUEHL, ANTON

Thirty prints. Processes and sizes vary.
Purchase.

"Chemical Tanks," 1927.
79:023:023

"Connecticut," 1926.
79:023:030

"Davits (?), Italy," 1929.
79:023:027

"Gas Works, Stamford, Conn.," 1927.
79:023:019

"Girl, Chair, Window," 1926.
79:023:018

"Italian Farmer," 1929.
79:023:020

"Male Model Ad for Weber and Heilbroner," 1929.
79:023:021

"Marlene Dietrich," n.d.
79:023:014

"Marlene Dietrich," n.d.
79:023:015

"Mexican Market," 1932.
79:023:001

"Mexican Potter," 1932.
79:023:005

"Nantucket," 1926.
79:023:029

"The Old Mill, Canaan, Conn.," 1924.
79:023:024

"Picket Fence," 1925.
79:023:026

Untitled, n.d. (Close-up of young girl's face.)
79:023:004

Untitled, n.d. (Group of young boys by pier.)
79:023:008

Untitled, n.d. (Woman with parasol.)
79:023:010

Untitled, n.d. (Marimba group.)
79:023:011

Untitled, n.d. (Woman pointing on fire escape.)
79:023:012

Untitled, n.d. (Girl with cigarette.)
79:023:013

Untitled, n.d. (Top hats.)
79:023:016

Untitled, n.d. (Woman kneeling with ballerina
    in background.)
79:023:022

Untitled, n.d. (Woman in shower.)
79:023:028

Untitled, 1926. (Large building with trees.)
79:023:009

Untitled, 1927. (Light bulbs.)
79:023:018

Untitled, 1929. (Trees.)
79:023:007

Untitled, 1932. (Two young Mexican girls.)
79:023:006

Untitled, 1935. (Young boy.)
79:023:002

"Waterfront," n.d.
79:023:025

"Woman and Child with Straw Hats," 1932.
79:023:003

BULLOCK, WYNN

"Wynn Bullock, Photographer," a 16 mm. film
by Thom Tyson.
Purchase.

CALLAHAN, HARRY

Collection of Harry Callahan

Stone, J.
"L.A. California," 1978.
Gelatin silver print. 20.2 x 30.3 cm.
Gift of Harry Callahan.
79:050:001

CALLIS, JO ANN

"Black Bands," 1977.
Type C print. 18.1 x 13.4 cm.
Special purchase.
79:031:005

"Black Sun Pictures #1," 1976.
Gelatin silver print. 32.7 x 41.9 cm.
Special purchase.
79:031:007

"Black Sun Picture #8," 1976.
Gelatin silver print. 32.7 x 42.0 cm.
Special purchase.
79:031:006

"Feet on Ottoman," 1976.
Gelatin silver print. 18.6 x 23.6 cm.
Special purchase.
79:031:001

Untitled, 1976. (From the *Morphe Series*.)
Gelatin silver print. 15.3 x 22.4 cm.
Special purchase.
79:031:002

Untitled, 1976. (From the *Morphe Series*.)
Gelatin silver print. 15.3 x 22.4 cm.
Special purchase.
79:031:003

Untitled, 1976. (From the *Morphe Series*.)
Gelatin silver print. 15.3 x 22.7 cm.
Special purchase.
79:031:004

Camp, Roger. See: ADAMS, ANSEL.
Collection of Ansel Adams.

Chapman, Neil. See: ADAMS, ANSEL.
Collection of Ansel Adams.

CHIARENZA, CARL

"Charleston 64," April, 1976.
Gelatin silver print. 24.4 x 31.1 cm.
Purchase.
79:025:001

"Fall River 19," February 1976.
Gelatin silver print. 23.6 x 30.6 cm.
Purchase.
79:025:003

"Fitchburg 20," February 1976.
Gelatin silver print. 23.6 x 31.2 cm.
Purchase.
79:025:002

"Gloucester 63A," 1963.
Gelatin silver print. 26.1 x 33.9 cm.
Gift of the photographer.
79:025:005

"Somerville 17," November 1975.
Gelatin silver print. 23.2 x 31.4 cm.
Purchase.
79:025:004

Day, J. L. See: ADAMS, ANSEL.
Collection of Ansel Adams.

DWORSKY, SUZANNE R.

"Cape Cod," 1978.
Type C print by Rick Mandelkorn. 24.5 x 35.0 cm.
Purchase.
79:041:001

"On the Beach," 1978.
Type C print by Rick Mandelkorn. 24.5 x 35.0 cm.
Purchase.
79:041:002

"Sea Breeze," 1978.
Type C print by Rick Mandelkorn. 24.5 x 34.4 cm.
Purchase.
79:041:003

Fantozzi, R. See: SISKIND, AARON.
Portraits of Aaron Siskind.

FRANK, JO ANN

"Circle #11," 1978.
Gelatin silver print. 20.1 x 25.2 cm.
Purchase.
79:018:002

"Homage to Duchamp," 1976–77.
Gelatin silver print. 19.3 x 24.2 cm.
Purchase.
79:018:001

"Vertical Ribbon," 1976.
Gelatin silver print; two images.
24.1 x 19.4 cm. each.
Purchase.
79:018:003–004

FRANK, ROBERT

"City Fathers — Hoboken, New Jersey," ca. 1956.
Gelatin silver print. 37.2 x 47.8 cm.
Gift of Mr. and Mrs. Harry H. Lunn, Jr.
79:045:004

"Detroit," 1954.
Gelatin silver print. 33.0 x 22.0 cm.
Gift of Mr. and Mrs. Harry H. Lunn, Jr.
79:045:006

"N.Y.C.," 1948.
Gelatin silver print. 24.6 x 17.8 cm.
Gift of Mr. and Mrs. Harry H. Lunn, Jr.
79:045:001

"New York City," 1951.
Gelatin silver print. 33.9 x 21.5 cm.
Gift of Mr. and Mrs. Harry H. Lunn, Jr.
79:045:002

"New York City Aquarium," 1956.
Gelatin silver print. 34.2 x 22.3 cm.
Gift of Mr. and Mrs. Harry H. Lunn, Jr.
79:045:005

"Paris," 1949–50.
Gelatin silver print. 28.7 x 19.3 cm.
Gift of Mr. and Mrs. Harry H. Lunn, Jr.
79:045:008

"Santa Fe, New Mexico," ca. 1956.
Gelatin silver print. 22.0 x 32.6 cm.
Gift of Mr. and Mrs. Harry H. Lunn, Jr.
79:045:009

"St. Nicholas Arena, N.Y.," 1954.
Gelatin silver print. 19.5 x 29.3 cm.
Gift of Mr. and Mrs. Harry H. Lunn, Jr.
79:045:007

"U.S. 91, Leaving Blackfoot, Idaho," 1955.
Gelatin silver print. 21.9 x 33.4 cm.
Purchase.
78:172:009

"Willem de Kooning," 1958.
Gelatin silver print. 33.0 x 21.8 cm.
Gift of Mr. and Mrs. Harry H. Lunn, Jr.
79:045:003

Fry, George, III. See: ADAMS, ANSEL.
Collection of Ansel Adams.

GOWIN, EMMET

Eighteen gelatin silver prints, except when
indicated. Sizes vary.
Special purchase, except where indicated.

"Barry, Dwayne and Turkeys,
Danville, Virginia," 1970.
79:061:011

"Chevaux De Friez and Fields, Innishmore,
Aran Islands, County Galway, Ireland," 1978.
(From the *Working Landscape* series.)
79:061:006

"Connor Pass, Dingle, County Kerry, Ireland," 1978.
(From the *Working Landscape* series.)
79:061:004

"Edith, Danville, Virginia," 1967.
79:061:010

"Edith, Danville, Virginia," 1971.
Gift of the photographer.
79:061:018

"Edith, Newton, Pa.," 1974.
Gift of the photographer.
79:061:017

"Family, Danville, Virginia," 1970.
79:061:012

"Fields (with hay bales), Glenshane Pass,
County Derry, Northern Ireland," 1977.
(From the *Working Landscape* series.)
Toned gelatin silver print.
Gift of the photographer.
79:061:001

"Garden, Siena, Italy," 1978.
(From the *Working Landscape* series.)
79:061:005

"Garden, Siena, Italy," 1978.
(From the *Working Landscape* series.)
79:061:007

"Garden, Siena, Italy," 1978.
(From the *Working Landscape* series.)
79:061:008

"Hog Butchering near Danville, Virginia," 1975.
79:061:016

"Nancy Wells (twine and blanket construction),
Danville, Virginia," 1971.
79:061:015

"Peat Cutting, Healey Pass,
County Kerry, Ireland," 1978.
(From the *Working Landscape* series.)
Gift of the photographer.
79:061:002

"Lock House Yard, Killalde,
County Clare, Ireland," 1978.
(From the *Working Landscape* series.)
Toned gelatin silver print.
Gift of the photographer.
79:061:003

"Rennie Booher (death portrait),
Danville, Virginia," 1972.
79:061:014

"Retired Potato Field, Achill Island,
County Mayo, Ireland," 1978.
(From the *Working Landscape* series.)
79:061:009

"Sheep Fleece, Yorkshire, England," 1972.
79:061:013

HAHN, BETTY

"Dried Flower," 1978.
Vandyke print; hand-colored with various media.
50.5 x 40.8 cm.
Special purchase.
79:058:003

"Large Blue Chrysanthemum #3," 1978.
Cyanotype; hand-colored with various media.
50.5 x 40.5 cm.
Special purchase.
79:058:001

"Red Rover on Gold," 1978.
Vandyke print; hand-colored with various media.
50.5 x 40.5 cm.
Special purchase.
79:058:002

HARNEY, THOM

"Old Friends," n.d.
Gelatin silver print. 22.0 x 33.0 cm.
Purchase.
79:043:002

"Puppy," n.d.
Gelatin silver print. 22.0 x 33.0 cm.
Purchase.
79:043:001

Hass, Kevin. See: ADAMS, ANSEL.
Collection of Ansel Adams.

HEINECKEN, ROBERT

Fourteen photographs.
Special purchase.

"Autographic Glove/Fabric," 1974.
Gelatin silver print. 15.9 x 24.0 cm.
79:010:001

"Breast/Bomb," 1967.
Gelatin silver prints; cut and reassembled.
38.1 x 38.1 cm.
79:046:004

"Cream Six," 1970.
Photographic emulsion on canvas; pastel chalk;
six units. 104.1 x 228.6 cm. total.
79:046:006

"Daytime Color TV Fantasy #5," 1974.
Four-color photographic lithograph.
16.8 x 22.2 cm.
79:046:002

"The Evolution of the Hair of the Artist, etc.," 1974.
Gelatin silver prints. 34.3 x 45.7 cm.
79:046:009

"14 or 15 Buffalo Ladies, #1 VIII," 1969.
Photographic lithograph; chalk; marking pen.
31.7 x 20.3 cm.
79:046:003

Just Good Eats for You Diner. (A set of eight
lithographs in plastic and vinyl menu folder.)
Lithographs. 25.3 x 20.3 cm. each.
79:009:001–008

"Le Voyeur/Robbe-Grillet #1," 1972.
Photographic emulsion on canvas; bleach;
pastel chalk. 33.0 x 66.0 cm.
79:046:010

"Mademoiselles — Dark," December 1969.
Offset lithograph. 24.8 x 24.8 cm.
79:010:002

"T is for Turkey Leg #1," 1971.
Gelatin silver print; photogram. 11.1 x 18.7 cm.
79:046:008

"TV Dinner/Shrimp," 1971.
Photographic emulsion on canvas formed with
pastel chalk and resin. 25.4 x 33.0 cm.
79:046:001

"Tribute to Glamour," 1966.
Positive transparency over magazine collage.
40.1 x 27.9 cm.
79:046:005

Untitled, May 1970.
Offset litho with pastel and pencil. 25.5 x 25.2 cm.
79:010:003

"Vary Cliche/Lesbianism 2/20," 1978.
Four color photographic lithograph. 56.0 x 71.2 cm.
79:046:007

Henningsen, Chuck. See: ADAMS, ANSEL.
Collection of Ansel Adams.

HYDE, PHILIP

"Dolores River Canyon, San Juan Rockies,
Colorado," 1974.
Dye transfer print. 25.1 x 33.2 cm.
Purchase.
79:039:002

"Wall Circle Cliffs, Utah," 1978.
Dye transfer print. 33.5 x 25.3 cm. (visible).
Purchase.
79:039:001

Jacobi, Lotte. See: STRAND, PAUL.
Portraits of Paul Strand.

JONES, HAROLD

" 'A' Mountain, Southwest," 1977.
Gelatin silver print. 33.4 x 41.4 cm.
Gift of the photographer.
78:033:021

"Curtain Rods and Hibachi," 1977.
Gelatin silver print. 33.3 x 41.5 cm.
Gift of the photographer.
78:033:024

"Gates Pass, South," 1977.
Gelatin silver print. 33.0 x 42.1 cm.
Gift of the photographer.
78:033:003

"Hang Gliding," 1977.
Gelatin silver print. 33.4 x 41.4 cm.
Gift of the photographer.
78:033:012

"Landscape (with Jack)," 1977.
Gelatin silver print. 33.0 x 42.1 cm.
Gift of the photographer.
78:033:026

"Patio," 1977.
Gelatin silver print. 33.4 x 41.3 cm.
Gift of the photographer.
78:033:006

"Sabino Canyon: Picnic," 1977.
Gelatin silver print. 38.6 x 47.8 cm.
Gift of the photographer.
78:033:032

"Still Life/Landscape with Olives," 1977.
Gelatin silver print. 33.3 x 41.6 cm.
Gift of the photographer.
78:033:023

"Still Life with Milk," 1977.
Gelatin silver print. 33.0 x 42.2 cm.
Gift of the photographer.
78:033:015

"Gates Pass, Looking Toward Tucson," 1976.
Gelatin silver print. 33.0 x 42.1 cm.
Gift of the photographer.
78:033:016

KANAGA, CONSUELA

"El Track, N.Y.C.," n.d.
Gelatin silver print. 17.3 x 12.3 cm.
Purchase.
79:059:001

McFARLAND, LAWRENCE

Untitled, April 1977.
    (Martha on Crane Beach, Mass.)
Gelatin silver print. 19.0 x 30.4 cm.
Purchase.
79:040:001

Untitled, April 1977. (Black Pyramid Hill
    near Rip Van Winkle Bridge, New York.)
Gelatin silver print. 19.0 x 30.4 cm.
Gift of the photographer.
79:040:004

Untitled, September 1977. (Kodak pointing
    toward McCoy, Colorado.)
Gelatin silver print. 19.0 x 30.5 cm.
Gift of the photographer.
79:040:003

Untitled, November 1977. (Flags on Rt. 22,
    New York.)
Gelatin silver print. 18.9 x 30.3 cm.
Purchase.
79:040:002

McGraw, Richard F. See: ADAMS, ANSEL.
    Collection of Ansel Adams.

Mandelkorn, Rick. See: DWORSKY, SUZANNE R.

MATHER, MARGRETHE

One hundred forty-six photographs by
    Margrethe Mather.
Platinum and gelatin silver prints. Sizes vary.
Purchase.
79:013:001–130; 79:017:001–016

Michele, Marion. See: STRAND, PAUL.
    Portraits of Paul Strand.

MOHR, JEAN

Two untitled portraits of W. Eugene Smith, 1958.
Gelatin silver prints. Sizes vary.
Gift of the photographer.
79:044:001–002

Two untitled portraits of Alfred Eisenstaedt.
Gelatin silver prints. 23.5 x 15.9 cm.
Gift of the photographer.
79:044:004

Muray, Nicholas. See: ROCHE, JOHN P.

PLOWDEN, DAVID

"F.D.R. Drive, New York City, N.Y.," n.d.
Gelatin silver print. 26.7 x 32.5 cm.
Purchase.
79:060:005

"From Cap Lumière, New Brunswick," n.d.
Gelatin silver print. 20.5 x 34.3 cm.
Purchase.
79:060:004

"House by Tracks, Lordville, New York," n.d.
Gelatin silver print. 27.2 x 29.2 cm.
Purchase.
79:060:001

"House — Newark, New York," n.d.
Gelatin silver print. 31.5 x 26.2 cm.
Purchase.
79:060:007

"Row of Houses, Anaconda, Montana," n.d.
Gelatin silver print. 26.8 x 27.0 cm.
Purchase.
79:060:003

"Street by Steel Mills, Johnstown, Pa.," n.d.
Gelatin silver print. 24.5 x 27.2 cm.
Purchase.
79:060:006

"Telephone Pole, Fergus County, Montana," n.d.
Gelatin silver print. 26.5 x 29.2 cm.
Purchase.
79:060:002

PORTER, ELIOT

Birds in Flight. (Portfolio.)
Santa Fe and New York: Bell Editions, 1978.
Dye transfer prints. Sizes vary.
Purchase.
79:014:001–008

RANKAITIS, SUSAN

Two untitled gelatin silver monoprints (toned and altered) from the series *Iconics,* ca. 1978.
Sizes vary.
Special purchase.
79:032:001–002

REXROTH, NANCY

"Angel of Mercy Nursing Home, Albany, Ohio," 1976.
Gelatin silver print. 10.0 x 10.1 cm.
Purchase.
79:011:001

"House, Pomeroy, Ohio," 1970.
Gelatin silver print. 10.1 x 10.4 cm.
Purchase.
79:011:003

"Winter Trees, Nelsonville, Ohio," 1976.
Gelatin silver print. 7.0 x 7.1 cm.
Purchase.
79:011:002

ROCHE, JOHN P.

"Hans von Kaltenborn, CBS News Commentator," n.d.
Carbro print of negative by Nicholas Muray.
33.2 x 26.4 cm.
Purchase.
79:002:002

"Tony Sarg, Internationally-known Artist and Designer," n.d.
Carbro print of negative by Nicholas Muray.
37.7 x 31.8 cm.
Purchase.
79:002:001

Ross, Alan. See: ADAMS, ANSEL.
Collection of Ansel Adams.

SCHAEFER, JOHN P.

"Waterfalls above the Rio Urique," n.d.
Special edition print accompanying the deluxe edition of the book *Tarahumara* by Bernard Fontana and John P. Schaefer.
Gelatin silver print. 22.6 x 17.7 cm.
Purchase.
79:026:001

SISKIND, AARON

Collection of Aaron Siskind.

Fantozzi, R.
"Arequipa," 1979. (Portrait of Aaron Siskind.)
Gelatin silver print. 1.0 x 16.8 cm.
Gift of Aaron Siskind.
79:022:001

SKOFF, GAIL

From the series, *Images of Bali,* 1976–77.

"Before the Cremation."
Gelatin silver print; hand-colored. 30.4 x 30.2 cm.
Special purchase.
79:053:005

"Cremation Animal."
Gelatin silver print; hand-colored. 30.4 x 28.6 cm.
Special purchase.
79:053:003

"Flaming Sarcophagus."
Gelatin silver print; hand-colored. 30.4 x 29.2 cm.
Special purchase.
79:053:004

"Oka & Sri."
Gelatin silver prints; hand-colored. 30.4 x 30.4 cm.
Special purchase.
79:053:001

"Trance Dancer."
Gelatin silver print; hand-colored. 30.4 x 30.4 cm.
Special purchase.
79:053:002

Stone, J. See: CALLAHAN, HARRY.
Collection of Harry Callahan.

Strand, Hazel Kingsbury. See: STRAND, PAUL.
Portraits of Paul Strand.

STRAND, PAUL

Portraits of Paul Strand
Twenty-seven portraits by anonymous, Susan Barron, Marion Michele, Lotte Jacobi, and Hazel Strand.
Gelatin silver prints. Sizes vary.
Gift of Hazel Strand.
79:004:001–010; 79:005:001–002; 79:006:001; 79:007:001–010

Tyson, Thom. See: BULLOCK, WYNN.

Upham, George. See: ADAMS, ANSEL.
Collection of Ansel Adams. (Signature illegible.)

VAN BLARCUM, ARTIE

Twelve gelatin silver prints. Sizes vary.
Gift of the photographer.

"Harbor Set," n.d.
79:012:002

"Harbour View, Thatcher's Island," n.d.
79:012:008

"Old Faithful," n.d.
79:012:012

"Pets be Friends," n.d.
79:012:011

"Time for a Short Puff," n.d.
79:012:001

"Tru Man," n.d.
79:012:010

"Two Part Harmony," n.d.
79:012:005

Untitled, n.d. (Man sweeping.)
79:012:003

"Water Frolic," n.d.
79:012:007

"Wing Pattern," n.d.
79:012:004

"Wings on the Maurice R., Port Morris,
New York," n.d.
79:012:009

"Winter on the Farm," n.d.
79:012:006

WESTON, BRETT

"Austrian Landscape," n.d.
Gelatin silver print. 19.3 x 24.2 cm.
Purchase.
79:054:001

WILSON, GEORGE WASHINGTON

"Rosslyn Chapel, Looking E.," n.d.
Albumen print. 20.6 x 13.2 cm.
Transfer from the University of Arizona
Art Department.
79:047:001

"Rosslyn Chapel, Roof," n.d.
Albumen print. 20.4 x 13.9 cm.
Transfer from the University of Arizona
Art Department.
79:047:002

YAVNO, MAX

Fourteen gelatin silver prints. Sizes vary.
Purchase.

"Army Street," n.d.
79:024:012

"Cable Car," n.d.
79:024:001

"Heiress," n.d.
79:024:003

"Keyboard Houses," n.d.
79:024:007

"Kuniyoshi," n.d.
79:024:011

"Leg," n.d.
79:024:005

"Lettuce Pickers," n.d.
79:024:004

"Muscle Beach," n.d.
79:024:002

"New York Snow Scene," n.d.
79:024:009

"S. Klein," n.d.
79:024:006

"Self Serve," n.d.
79:024:013

"Tenement/Clothesline," n.d.
79:024:010

"Two Chinese Men," n.d.
79:024:014

"View from Twin Peaks," n.d.
79:024:008

W. EUGENE SMITH
A Chronological Bibliography
1934–1979

Part I

The first portion of this bibliography, covering the years 1934 to 1951, is published in this issue of the journal, *Center for Creative Photography*. The remaining portion of the bibliography will be published in a forthcoming issue of the journal.

Introduction

THE PHOTOGRAPHS AND IDEAS of W. Eugene Smith have affected thousands of individuals all over the world. He has, as well, influenced several generations of photographers and his work has had a decided impact upon the face of the history of photography.

Smith was a working photographer for more than forty years. His own photographs and writings as well as commentary from others about his artistry have appeared in hundreds of publications during those years. This is a serious attempt to present a complete bibliography of these articles and other references. As such, it must inevitably fail. I know of the existence of articles that I could not verify, just as I know that there must exist other references unknown to me. Further research will always turn up more examples of the work of this extremely active artist. Yet I hope to present here an adequate tool that may be used by those who wish to build a more coherent understanding of the nature and range of W. Eugene Smith's life and career. And, as Smith's career has helped to define some of the boundaries of certain approaches to the expressive uses of photography, this bibliography might be useful to a fuller understanding of the growth of some of the ideas and concepts in play throughout several decades of photographic history. Thus, the references are arranged in chronological order, to provide a sense of the development of Smith's reputation as well as a sense of the context within which that reputation and influence developed. Given that aim, I have included references to those articles wherein Smith is merely mentioned or used as an exemplar, as well as those references that deal with his work in more depth. Since the bibliography, thus constituted, has become unwieldy (even if necessarily so) I have also included annotations to the more extensive and useful references.

Finally, a note of warning. Naturally, I began this bibliography by drawing from materials contained in the W. Eugene Smith Archive at the Center for Creative Photography at the University of Arizona in Tucson, Arizona. However, the Smith Archive contains only a portion of the materials mentioned in this bibliography and the presence of a reference in the bibliography does not necessarily mean that the original source is available from the Archive at the Center.

While it may seem presumptuous to append a statement of appreciation to a simple bibliography, nevertheless I am deeply indebted to the kind assistance of many people and I would like to thank them for their valuable and necessary help.

Let me thank Jim Enyeart, the director of the Center, who supported the project and who found the money for its publication; Minnette Burges, whose patience in the face of my random ways certainly extended beyond her professional responsibilities as editor; and Giles Wolak and Mary Lewis, who typed heroically.

I would like to thank Shigeru Miyagawa of the Department of Oriental Studies at the University of Arizona for his crucial translations of the Japanese language references and Aileen Smith for her assistance with them as well. Ms. Widger at the George Eastman House in Rochester, N.Y. somehow made the time to respond promptly to some formerly unresolvable problems and I'm grateful and I would like to thank Ramiro Fernandez at the Museum of Modern Art for his help. Jim and Evelyn Hughes in New York gave me a number of additional references culled from their own exhaustive research and I would like to acknowledge both their courtesy and their assistance.

I want to most particularly thank Cynthia Bower, of the University of Arizona Library, who clearly recognizing the most serious need at the time, volunteered her help to type a large portion of the manuscript. Cynthia, a professional librarian, has skills and talents far in excess to those she contributed here, and I can only be grateful for her willingness to perform this mundane but absolutely vital service for the project. And finally, thanks to my wife, Susan E. Cohen, who took many hours from her own valuable research time, to verify many references for me in libraries older and larger than I had access to at the time.

WILLIAM JOHNSON
April 1980

Notes on the Use of This Bibliography

This bibliography is divided by year and then into the categories *Books*, *Portfolios*, *Exhibition Catalogs*, and *Periodicals*. Newspaper references are included with *Periodicals*. References are then arranged alphabetically by title within each section within each year.

Two basic forms of reference are used here. The first is in the more-or-less traditional format of title, author, magazine title, pagination and so on. This form was used when the Smith material constituted the major portion of the content of that article — either as illustration or as the subject. The second form of reference begins with the number of photographs, then, in parentheses, the subject of the photograph or the essay in which the photograph appeared, followed by page number and the remainder of the reference. This second form was used when the Smith material constituted only a portion of the total material in the reference. While this alternation in form may at first appear to be confusing, it provides a far more accurate indicator of the true nature of the reference.

W. Eugene Smith began making photographs while he was in high school in Kansas during the mid-thirties. Some of this work was published in various school publications and yearbooks. He also had some photographs published in the local newspapers (*The Wichita Eagle* and *The Wichita Beacon*) during those years. In addition to this, he stated in interviews that some of his photographs taken of the Kansas drought of 1934 were published in the *The New York Times*. During this period the photographer was rarely credited; however, I have included several possible or probable references from *The New York Times*.

———————————1934———————————

PERIODICALS

New York Times

[Possible.] "In a Land Made Desolate By Drought. A Vivid Picture of a World Transformed, Where High Courage Keeps Hopes Alive," by H.L. Robbins. *New York Times* (New York, N.Y.) (Sun. July 22, 1934), Magazine Section 6, pp. 4-5. 5 b&w by various photographers.
[Photographs credited to Associated Press, Times Wide World and E. Anthony Armstrong].

[Probable.] 1 b&w (Arkansas River Dried Up by Drought) *New York Times*, (Wed. July 25, 1934), Section 1, p.3.

———————————1936———————————

PERIODICALS

Wichita Eagle

1 portrait plus caption in: "To Enroll at Notre Dame." *Wichita Eagle* (Wichita, Kan.) (Sept. 13, 1936). p. [n.p.].
[Portrait of Smith with camera, caption stating that he will work his way through Notre Dame by photographing.]

After attending Notre Dame University briefly — and photographing there intensively — Smith went to New York and worked for *Newsweek* magazine for the final months of 1937 and first part of 1938. Once again published photographs were not credited to Smith, and the *Newsweek* references are based on either his (incomplete) scrapbooks or on some of the images that remain in his collection. He claimed to have destroyed a great many of his early negatives and prints, however, and it is possible that these references are incomplete.

PERIODICALS

Newsweek

"New Business: The New Haven Railroad's Husking Bee." *Newsweek*, vol. 10, no. 18 (Nov. 1, 1937), pp. 34-35. 8 b&w.

"Horse Show." *Newsweek*, vol. 10, no. 20 (Nov. 15, 1937), p. 27. 6 b&w. [1 b&w credited to Acme, 5 credited to Newsphotos. 1 definitely by Smith, other 4 highly probable.]

Photographic Digest

[Probable.] 1 b&w ("Under the El") *The Photographic Digest*, vol. 3, no. 4 (Sept. 1937 [?]). p. [n.p.]
[Damaged reference: the photo was published in a Sept. issue of the *Photographic Digest*, and it is highly probable that the year is 1937, but I have been unable to verify the issue. — W.J.]

1 b&w (The Swan) *Photographic Digest*, vol. 3, no. 5 (Oct. 1937), p. 282.
[Credited to Eugene Smith.]

From late 1938 to 1943 Smith worked primarily as a free lance photographer associated with the Black Star photo agency. This time might be characterized as a period of hectic activity, enormous energy and a somewhat scattered focus. Smith would apparently (and seemingly did) go anywhere at any time to take a picture. And the Black Star agency, with its world wide contacts, would get those pictures published somewhere.

In addition to the references cited here from *American Magazine, Click, Colliers, Coronet, Cue, Friday, Life, Look, Ken, P.M., Parade, Pic, Time*, etc., and the many daily or weekly newspapers, Smith also had work published abroad in England (*Illustrated, Picture Post*), in France, Denmark (*Billed-Bladet*), Holland (*ABC*), Sweden (*Se*), South America (*La Prensa*), and Australia (*Yaffa*). He also sold work to individual companies for publicity or promotion. All in all, an enormously active period during his career.

This work was usually presented as single images, or a small group of images loosely clustered around a simple theme. Very few of these images are, in themselves, exceptional — although they certainly often display the sense of vitality, energy and technical skill that made Smith his early reputation. Taken as a group, however, a very large and complex body of work begins to emerge from this period. It is also apparent from Smith's photographic files that very often fifty or more photographs from each topic were made and printed for every single picture that was published in these magazines. Smith's mother claimed in 1945 that he made about 50,000 negatives before the war. While that number of negatives has not survived in the W. Eugene Smith Archive at the Center for Creative Photography, it may have been possible.

Again during this period many of the magazines would not credit the photographer. I have had, upon occasion, to guess at the reference. I have used three major sources of information for this section of the bibliography — Smith's photo files, his scrapbooks and tear sheets, and some fragmentary business records from the Black Star agency. All of these are incomplete, but by fitting them together and extensive searching through magazines and microfilms, I have located at least a representative portion of his published work from this period. When I am certain of a reference (a known image from the collection or a credit line) then the reference is presented here as it is; when I have reason to believe (from documentary evidence or whatever) that a non-credited Smith reference exists, the notation 'Possible' or 'Probable' appears.

PERIODICALS

American Magazine

"America's Interesting People: Hostess."
American Magazine, vol. 126, no. 2 (Aug.
1938), p. 87. 2 b&w.
[Hospital aide Mrs. Wilfred Funk.]

"America's Interesting People: Cops."
American Magazine, vol. 126, no. 6 (Dec.
1938), pp. 92-93. 6 b&w.
[19-year-old Roy Bassette, Jr., founder of the
Tri-State Detective Agency.]

Ken

1 b&w (Cancer patient) on p. 53 in: "What
of the Knife?" by Martin Lewis.
Ken, vol 2 no. 12, Whole number 12 (Dec.
15, 1938), pp. 72-75. 11 b&w photographs
by various photographers on pp. 48-53.
[Credited to Newsphotos, this photograph is
identical to one published earlier in the Mar.
28, 1938 Newsweek. The article is about
discoveries in medical technology.]

Life

1 b&w (Old couple) on p. 66 in: "Old Age."
Life, vol. 5, no. 19 (Nov. 7, 1938), pp. 56-66.
22 b&w by various photographers.

2 b&w (Soldiers in gas masks) on p. 57 in:
"Rearmament." *Life*, vol.5, no. 25 (Dec. 19,
1938), pp. 44-57. 44 b&w by various
photographers.

"Life Goes to a Rubber Ball." *Life*, vol. 5, no.
26 (Dec. 26, 1938), pp. 56-58. 10 b&w.
[Costume ball in Akron, Ohio.]

Newsweek

[Probable.] "American Silk." *Newsweek*,
vol. 11, no. 10 (Mar. 7, 1938), p. 32. 5 b&w.
[John Ousta of N.Y.C. raised silkworms in
his attic. Photographs similar to these are in
the W. Eugene Smith Archive.]

"Science and Medicine: Cancer: Medicine
Reports Its Progress in Centuries-Old Search
for Cure." *Newsweek*, vol. 11, no. 13 (Mar.
28, 1938), pp. 22-23. 3 b&w.

"Entertainment: Gargantua the Great:
Young Fellow of 7 is the Star of New
Ringling Circus." *Newsweek*, vol. 11, no. 15
(Apr. 11, 1938), p. 21. 4 b&w.
[1 credited to Doulens, 3 credited to News-
photos are by Smith.]

1 b&w (Actor Rex Ingram in "Haiti") on
p. 25 in: "Entertainment: Theatre Week. A
Government in Greasepaint," by George
Jean Nathan. *Newsweek*, vol. 11, no. 16
(Apr. 18, 1938).

Philadelphia Inquirer

[Probable.] "Grandma's Home-Made Beauty
Tricks Work Wonders for the Modern Miss:
An egg tones up the scalp and oatmeal paste
aids that schoolgirl complexion." *Phila-
delphia Inquirer. Everybody's Weekly and
Picture Parade* (Philadelphia, Pa.), (Sun.,
Sept. 25, 1938), p: 3. 6 b&w credited to
Black Star.

Picture Post (London)

"What a Girl Should Do in a Taxi". *Picture
Post* (London), (Nov. 12, 1938), pp. [n.p.]. 7
b&w.
[Physical exercises inside a taxicab.]

Scribner's Magazine

1 b&w (Artist A. Kyrometes) on p. 29 in:
"Life in the U. S., ... Photographic."
Scribner's Magazine, vol. 104, no. 3 (Sept.
1938), pp. 29-33. 5 b&w by various
photographers.

PERIODICALS

American Magazine

"America's Interesting People: Daters." *American Magazine*, vol. 127, no. 4 (Apr. 1939), p. 101. 1 b&w.
[Celebrity service. Ted Strong & Earl Blackwell.]

"America's Interesting People: Bikesmith." *American Magazine*, vol. 127, no. 4 (Apr. 1939), p. 103. 1 b&w.
[Bike tire maker Virginia Bailey.]

Billed-Bladet (Copenhagen)

"Vil Adressaten Fole Sig Ramt?" *Billed-Bladet* (Copenhagen), 2. Aargang Nr. 50 (Dec. 12, 1939), p. 2. 4 b&w.
[Rocket experimenters.]

Click

"A Taxi 'Gym' Helps Busy Stenographers to Reduce." *Click*, vol. 1, no. 12 (Jan. 1939), p. 26. 6 b&w.
[Health exercises in a taxi.]

"She Saved Broadway from the World's Fair." *Click*, vol. 2, no. 10 (Nov. 1939), pp. 10-11. 10 b&w plus color cover.
[Singer Carmen Miranda.]

Colliers

"Wade Down South," by Jack Wade. *Colliers*, vol. 104, no. 16 (Oct. 14, 1939), pp. 11, 96-97. 1 b&w.
[Duke University football coach Wallace Wade.]

Coronet

1 b&w (Bike tire maker Virginia Pye Bailey) on p. 163 in: "A Portfolio of Personalities." *Coronet*, vol. 5, no. 5, whole no. 29 (Mar. 1, 1939), pp. 158-164. 6 b&w by various photographers.

Cue

1 b&w (Singer Carmen Miranda) on front cover of *Cue*, vol. 8, no. 4 (July 22, 1939).

1 b&w (Dancer Ann Miller) on front cover of *Cue*, vol. 8, no. 16 (Oct. 14, 1939).
[Credit: Black Star.]

1 b&w (Harlem Jewish Rabbi W.A. Matthew) on p. 19 in: "Manhattan's Many Gods," by Henry P. Malmgreen. *Cue*, vol. 8, no. 21 (Nov. 18, 1939), pp. 18-19. 3 b&w by various photographers.
[2 by F.P.G., 1 by Black Star, Smith.]

"From Flowers to Dali," by Harold Wheaton. *Cue*, vol. 8, no. 23 (Dec. 2, 1939), pp. 18-19. 5 b&w.
[Wallpaper manufacturing.]

House and Garden

4 b&w on p. 36 in: "Commuter Parking," by Carl Feiss. *House and Garden*, vol. 76, no. 4 (Oct. 1939), Section 1, pp. 36, 74, 79. 4 b&w credited to Black Star (Smith portraying the commuter), plus 1 b&w by Gottscho of a commuter station at Valley Stream, N.Y.

Ken

3 b&w (Girl exercising) on p. 33 in: "Exercises in Exercise." *Ken*, vol. 4, no. 9 Whole no. 35 (June 1, 1939), pp. 31-37. 18 b&w by Morse-Pix, Anders, Black Star, Globe, European.
[Three photos from Smith's series "Exercises in a Taxicab" within a larger essay on exercise.]

Life

[NOTE: The Aperture monograph *W. Eugene Smith, His Photographs and Notes* (1969) contains an exceptionally fine bibliography on the photographs published in *Life* magazine. This bibliography was apparently gathered by exhaustively checking the credit boxes of each issue of *Life* magazine from 1938 through 1954. However, from 1939 through 1942 the Aperture bibliography credits a number of references to Smith that were credited in *Life* to "Eugene Smith — Cincinnati Post" rather than "W. Eugene Smith — Black Star." While I have not yet been able to verify the existence of another Eugene Smith who worked for the Cincinnati Post, the absence of substantiating photographs from the W. Eugene Smith Archive leads me to believe that these photographs are not by W. Eugene Smith. Therefore, I have not included those references in this bibliography.]

"Voder, the Machine that Talks like a Man, Duplicates the Human Throat." *Life*, vol. 6, no. 5 (Jan. 30, 1939), p. 24. 1 b&w, 2 illus.
[Portrait of woman operator at keyboard at the voder.]

"Life Goes to the Butlers' Ball." *Life*, vol. 6, no. 5 (Jan. 30, 1939), pp. 58-61. 22 b&w.
[Butlers' dance in New York City.]

1 b&w (Thomas Dewey at Republican banquet) on p. 65 in: "People." *Life*, vol. 6, no. 9 (Feb. 27, 1939), pp. 64-65. 5 b&w by various photographers.

1 b&w (Rightist political lecturer, Russell Dunn) on p. 61 in: "Fascism in America." *Life*, vol. 6, no. 10 (Mar. 6, 1939), pp. 57-63. 22 b&w by various photographers, 7 illus.

1 b&w (Propeller shafts being constructed at the Federal Shipbuilding Yard, Kearney, N.J.) on p. 22 in: "The U. S. Enjoys its Biggest Shipbuilding Boom Since World War." *Life*, vol. 6, no. 13 (Mar. 27, 1939), pp. 22-23. 5 b&w by various photographers.

1 b&w (Portrait of Pablo Prida, Mexican movie exhibitor) on p. 74; 2 b&w (Minister Luis Quintonilla and Cpt. Borzanza) on p. 75 in: "Latin American Diplomats Crowd Opening of 'Juarez'." *Life*, vol. 6, no. 19 (May 8, 1939), pp. 74-75. 6 b&w by various photographers.

"Maryland Schoolboys Crack Skulls and Shins in a Rough Game of Lacrosse." *Life*, vol. 6, no. 22 (May 29, 1939), p. 57. 6 b&w.

"The Raising of the 'Squalus'." *Life*, vol. 6, no. 24 (June 12, 1939), pp. 27-29. 4 b&w, 1 illus.
[Raising sunken submarine.]

"Theatre: Daniel Webster Outwits a Boston Devil in a New American Folk Opera." *Life*, vol. 6, no. 24 (June 12, 1939), pp. 37-38, 40. 9 b&w.
[Staged performance of *The Devil and Daniel Webster.*]

1 b&w (Gov. Wm. H. Vanderbilt of Rhode Island in carriage) on p. 22 in: "Republican Record Since 1938 Gives Clue to Republican Behavior in 1941." *Life*, vol. 6, no. 25 (June 19, 1939), pp. 22-23. 10 b&w by various photographers.

2 b&w (New York World's Fair) on p. 55 in: "Life at the World's Fair." *Life*, vol. 7, no.1 (July 3, 1939), pp. 54-69. 59 b&w by various photographers.

"World's First Autogiro Air-Mail Service Starts at Philadelphia." *Life*, vol. 7, no. 3 (July 17, 1939), p. 20. 2 b&w.

"Theatre: Broadway Likes Miranda's Piquant Portuguese Songs." *Life*, vol. 7, no. 3 (July 17, 1939), p. 34. 1 b&w.
[Singer Carmen Miranda.]

2 b&w (Portraits of actor Clifton Webb, actress Libby Holman) on p. 58 in: "Summer Theatre." *Life*, vol. 7, no. 5 (July 31, 1939), pp. 50-60. 32 b&w by various photographers.

"Australia May Well Lift Davis Cup." *Life*, vol. 7, no. 6 (Aug. 7, 1939), pp. 22-23. 12 b&w by Smith, 2 b&w by other photographers.
[Tennis star Adrian Quist.]

1 b&w (Dancer Irene Castle) on p. 19 in: "Life on the Newsfronts of the World: Picture of the Week." *Life*, vol. 7, no. 8 (Aug. 21, 1939), p. 19.

5 b&w (Dancer Ann Miller) in: "The Week the War Began", by Noel F. Busch. *Life*, vol. 7, no. 12 (Sept. 18, 1939), pp. 74-76, 78-81. 57 b&w by various photographers.

"Science: Technicians Design Model Rockets Hoping for Transatlantic Flight." *Life*, vol. 7, no. 15 (Oct. 9, 1939), pp. 37-40. 7 b&w.

1 b&w (Mildred Burns of St. Albins, Long Island) on p. 96 in: "Bill Stern, Top NBC Announcer Picks His 1939 All-American Team." *Life*, vol. 7, no.21 (Nov. 20, 1939), pp. 94-97. 14 b&w by various photographers.
[Burns is an admirer of Notre Dame end Bud Kerr.]

1 b&w (Betty Grable) on front cover of *Life*, vol. 7, no. 24 (Dec. 11, 1939).

Look

"A Boy and His Dog." *Look*, vol. 3, no. 4 (Feb. 14, 1939), pp. 14-15. 6 b&w.
[Dog hit by car, cared for by the A.S.P.C.A.]

"Broadway starts the Season with 'The Man Who Came to Dinner.' New Kaufman-Hart Play Takes Alexander Woolcott for a Ride." *Look*, vol. 3 (Nov. 21, 1939), pp. 60-61. 7 b&w by various photographers.
[Credits: pp. 60-61. Richard Tucker, Jr., W. Eugene Smith - Black Star, Acme, Culver Service.]

New York Times

1 b&w (Singer Carmen Miranda), *New York Times*. (New York, N.Y.) (Sun. Aug. 6, 1939), Section 9, p. 2.

1 b&w (Camouflaged artillery gun) on p. 19 in: "Camouflage Mysteries," by Daniel Lang. *New York Times*. (New York, N.Y.) (Sun. Oct. 8, 1939) Magazine Section 7, p. 19. 3 b&w.
[Credit: Times-Wide World, Black Star.]

"Carnival on Ice." *New York Times*. (New York, N.Y.) (Sun. Dec. 3, 1939). Rotogravure Picture Section 8, p. 2. 5 b&w.
[Credit: 4, W. Eugene Smith; 1, Moulin.]

St. Louis Post Dispatch Pictures.

"Colored Jews of Harlem." *St. Louis Post-Dispatch Pictures*. (St. Louis, Mo.) (Sun. Jan. 8, 1939), pp. [n.p.]. 8 b&w.

Se (Stockholm)

"Sporting Dans: Baletten Dansar Pa Skridsko." *Se* (Stockholm), no. 27, [n.d. c.1939], pp. 30-31 [?]. 9 b&w.
[Ice skating show.]

1 b&w (U. S. Army soldier in gas mask) on cover of *Se* (Stockholm) no. 37 (Sept. 8-12, 1939).

Time

1 b&w (Actress Grace McDonald) on p. 60
in: "New Musical in Manhattan." *Time*, vol.
34, no. 22 (Nov. 27, 1939), p. 60.
[Actress Grace McDonald in "Very Warm
for May".]

U.S. Camera

1 b&w (Army cheerleaders at Notre Dame
— Army football game) *U.S. Camera 1940*
(1939), p. 207.

————————————— 1940 —————————————

BOOKS

"The Army of the United States.", presented
by Morris Sheppard. Senate Document no.
91. 76th Congress, 1st Session. Washington:
Govt. Printing Office, 1940. 200 p. 166 b&w
by various photographers.
[Smith credited in back but individual
photographs not credited; Smith possibles
on pp. 31, 130, 131, 132, 134. Chemical
Warfare Service.]

PERIODICALS

American Magazine

"America's Interesting People: Tubist."
American Magazine, vol. 129, no. 4 (Apr.
1940), p. 78. 1 b&w.
[Neon tube designer Edward Seise.]

"America's Interesting People: Landlord."
American Magazine, vol. 130, no. 4 (Oct.
1940), p. 74. 1 b&w.
[Landlord Harry Suchin.]

Billed-Bladet (Copenhagen)

"I Sikker Havn." *Billed-Bladet* (Copenhagen), 3. Aargang, no. 14 (Mar. 28, 1940 [?]),
[n.p., 1 page]. 2 b&w.
[Ocean liner Queen Elizabeth docking in
N.Y. harbor.]

Collier's

"Ballerina Without Accent," by Quentin
Reynolds. *Collier's*, vol. 105, no. 5 (Feb. 3,
1940), pp. 16, 46. 1 b&w.
[Ballerina Nana Gollner.]

"More Than Base Hits," by Robert A. "Red"
Rolfe. *Collier's*, vol. 106, no. 7 (Aug. 17,
1940), pp. 13, 40. 1 b&w.
[N.Y. Yankee third baseman Red Rolfe.]

"Tennis Cinderella," by Arthur Mann.
Collier's, vol. 106, no. 10 (Sept. 7, 1940), pp.
19-20. 1 b&w.
[Tennis star Helen Bernhard.]

"Inside Wilkie's Head," by Congressman
Bruce Barton. *Collier's* vol. 106, no. 12
(Sept. 21, 1940), pp. 15,67,70. 1 b&w.
[Politician Wendell Wilkie.]

"Hi, Jinx!" by Luther Davis & John
Cleveland. *Collier's*, vol. 106, no. 15 (Oct.
12, 1940), pp. 11, 80. 1 color.
[Fashion model Jinx Falkenberg.]

"Plaids Please," by Henry L. Jackson.
Collier's, vol. 106, no. 15 (Oct. 12, 1940), p.
19. 4 color.
[Golf fashions for men.]

"The All-American Football Team," by
Grantland Rice. *Collier's*, vol. 106, no. 24
(Dec. 14, 1940), pp. 12-14, 71. 4 color, 4
b&w.

"Russian Genius," by Luther Davis and John Cleveland. *Collier's*, vol. 106, no. 26 (Dec. 28, 1940), pp. 22, 36. 1 b&w.
[Dancer George Balanchine.]

Coronet

1 b&w (Violinist Lucy Nielson) on p. 112 in: "A Portfolio of Personalities." *Coronet*, vol. 7, no. 5, whole no. 41 (Mar. 1, 1940), pp. 108-114. 6 b&w by various photographers.

Everyday Photography

1 b&w (Symbols of the sea) on p. 26; 1 b&w (Tears of the innocent) on p. 28 in: "Photo Forum." *Everyday Photography*, vol. 3, no. 5 (Jan. 1940), pp. 25-32, 15 b&w by various photographers.

"News Photography's Prodigy," by Roger Monsell. *Prize Photography* [*Everyday Photography*], vol. 5, no. 3 (Nov. 1940), pp. 12-13, 54-55. 4 b&w, 1 portrait.
[This is the first extended written commentary on Smith. It is written in an informal, semi-interview, enthusiastic style that focuses on his work experiences and methods, tells of his early high school interests, how he began to work commercially, and how he began to be successful. Strong emphasis is placed on his enormous energy and enthusiasm, as well as his technical skills.]

Friday

1 b&w (Singer Carmen Miranda) on cover of *Friday*, vol. 1, no. 1 (Mar. 15, 1940).

Hartford Newsdaily

"Religion: The Colored Jews Trace Ancestry to Solomon." *Hartford Newsdaily* (Hartford, Conn.) (May 9, 1940), p. 13. 6 b&w.

Illustrated (London)

"These Men are a World Problem." *Illustrated* (London), vol. 1, no. 52 (Feb. 24, 1940), pp. 18-21. 8 b&w by Smith, 5 b&w portraits.
[*"Illustrated* goes to Ellis Island to show you the interned crew of scuttled Nazi liner 'Columbus'."]

"British Children in America." *Illustrated* (London), vol. 2, no. 25 (Aug. 17, 1940), pp. 3-7. 15 b&w.

"Juliana in Canada." *Illustrated*, vol. 2, no. 36 (Nov. 2, 1940), pp. 10-12. 7 b&w.
[Princess Juliana in exile in Canada.]

Life

"This Weeks Events: Cromwells Arrive in Ottawa and Take Over U.S. Legation." *Life*, vol. 8, no. 6 (Feb. 5, 1940), p. 24. 4 b&w.
[U.S. Minister to Canada James H. R. Cromwell.]

"Picture of the Week: Francis Biddle, new Solicitor General climbs to his Department of Justice office past his own likeness in mural by his brother, George." *Life*, vol. 8, no. 8 (Feb. 19, 1940), p. 23. 1 b&w.

"Astronomy: Mercury, Mars, Saturn, Jupiter and Venus Line Up as Evening Stars." *Life*, vol. 8, no. 9 (Feb. 26, 1940), pp. 33-34. 3 b&w.

"Theatre: Betty Hutton Rips into Miss Muffet." *Life*, vol. 8, no. 11 (Mar. 11, 1940), p. 51. 12 b&w.

"Queen Elizabeth. World's Biggest Ship Crosses Sea to Safe Berth in New York Harbor." *Life*, vol. 8, no. 12 (Mar. 18, 1940), pp. 30-31. 1 b&w by Smith, 2 b&w by various photographers.

"This Week's Events: Milwaukee's Lyric Mayor Lifts His Voice in Song on Day of Inauguration." *Life*, vol. 8, no. 18 (Apr. 29, 1940), p. 35. 1 b&w.
[Mayor Carl Zeidler.]

"Sports: Girl Swimmers from New York Set New World's Medley Relay Record." *Life*, vol. 8, no. 18 (Apr. 29, 1940), pp. 69-70. 6 b&w.

"This Week's Events: Moe Annenberg Pleads Guilty of Biggest Tax-Evasion Job on Record." *Life*, vol. 8, no. 19 (May 6, 1940), p. 36. 1 b&w.

"Education: Psychology Professor Hypnotizes Student in Class Demonstration." *Life*, vol. 8, no. 21 (May 20, 1940), pp. 78-80. 7 b&w.
[Harold A. Swenson, University of Chicago.]

"Oil in Illinois: Rigs Rise Over Field and Farm as Boom Unlocks a New U.S. Frontier." *Life*, vol. 8, no. 24 (June 10, 1940), pp. 62-66. 10 b&w.
[Centralia — Salem, Illinois oil field.]

"Modern Living: Roller-Skate Dancing Starts a Bloomers Fad." *Life*, vol. 9, no. 2 (July 8, 1940), pp. 68-69. 4 b&w.

"This Week's Events: U.S. Opens its Homes and Heart to Refugee Children of England." *Life*, vol. 9, no. 4 (July 22, 1940), pp. 11-15. 7 b&w by Smith, 9 by various photographers.

"Medicine: U.S. Army Doctors Investigate the Punishment a Pilot Takes in Flight." *Life*, vol. 9, no. 4 (July 22, 1940), pp. 34, 36-38. 8 b&w by Smith, 2 by various photographers, 1 illus.

"Army Uses Tower to Train its New Parachute Troops." *Life*, vol. 9, no. 8 (Aug. 19, 1940), pp. 18-19. 3 b&w plus 1 b&w on cover.

1 b&w (Port Churchill, Manitoba) in: "Canada: One-half of North America Joins the Other on Defense." *Life*, vol. 9, no. 11 (Sept. 9, 1940), pp. 103-116. 60 b&w by various photographers, 20 illus.

4 b&w (U.S.S. Constellation) on pp. 52-54; 4 b&w (U.S. Naval War College) on pp. 59-60, 62; 3 b&w on p. 90 (Corn Belt Destroyer); 1 b&w on p. 92 (San Juan, Puerto Rico Naval Base); plus 1 b&w on front cover in: "The Navy: A Close-Up of the U.S. Navy." *Life*, vol. 9, no. 18 (Oct. 28, 1940), pp. 23-102. 134 b&w by various photographers.

"The Campaign: Americans Hit New High in Political Pep as Presidential Race Nears Finish." *Life*, vol. 9, no. 19 (Nov. 4, 1940), p. 23. 1 b&w.

1 b&w (Men waiting to be drafted) on p. 31 in: "The Draft: America Begins Training First Conscript Army in its Peacetime History." *Life*, vol. 9, no. 24 (Dec. 9, 1940), pp. 27-31. 40 b&w by various photographers.

"Ribald 'Tobacco Road' Has Seventh Broadway Birthday." *Life*, vol. 9, no. 25 (Dec. 16, 1940), p. 30. 8 b&w.

4 b&w (Dutch Princess Juliana and her children) on pp. 88-89 in: "Refugees: Children of Europe are America's Wards." *Life*, vol. 9, no. 25 (Dec. 16, 1940), pp. 88-95. 20 b&w by various photographers.

Look

1 b&w (Paul McNutt) on p. 17 which has been montaged to portrait of John Garner (by a different photographer) and a second McNutt portrait on p. 20 in: "Garner vs. McNutt," by Ernest K. Lindley. *Look*, vol. 4 (Feb. 13, 1940), pp. 17-21. 17 b&w by various photographers.
[Politicians John Garner, Paul McNutt possible presidential candidates.]

Medical Economics

1 b&w (The Capitol Building, Washington, D.C., after dark) Cover of *Medical Economics.* vol. 18, no. 2 (Nov. 1940).

Minicam

[Probable.] 1 b&w (Anchor chain) on p. 31 in: "Rhythm in Pictures. Types of Repetition and How to Put Them in Your Pictures," by S. J. Ressetar. *Minicam*, vol. 3, no. 12 (Aug. 1940), pp. 30-31. 6 b&w, 4 diagrams.

New York Times

"South of the Border — On Broadway," by Maurice Zolotow. *New York Times.* (New York, N.Y.) (Sun., Feb. 18, 1940). Magazine Section 7, p. 11. 3 b&w, 2 by Smith.
[Singer Carmen Miranda, dancer Diosa Costello in "Streets of Paris."]

Picture Post (London)

"Ice Follies of 1940." *Picture Post*, vol. 6, no. 10 (Mar. 9, 1940), p. 46. 3 b&w.

P.M.'s Weekly

[Probable.] "Nature: Invader From Japan Marches Right Along," by Margaret Bourke-White. *P.M.'s Weekly*, vol. 1, no. 7 (Aug. 4, 1940), Section Two, pp. 42-43. 5 b&w of Japanese beetles.
[This is a column under Margaret Bourke-White's name; often her photographs receive a separate credit line, not in this issue. Two photographs on p. 43 by Smith are in the W. Eugene Smith Archive.]

Popular Photography

1 b&w (Actor Burt Lahr) on p. 78; Smith mentioned on p. 144 in: "Prize Winning Pictures in the Popular Photography 1940 Picture Contest." *Popular Photography*, vol. 7, no. 6 (Dec. 1940), pp. 48-78, 142-144. 40 b&w by various photographers.
[Smith won the 22nd prize.]

La Prensa (Buenos Aires)

"Servicio Postal Norte Americano de Autogiros..." *La Prensa* (Buenos Aires), (April 28, 1940), Section 4, n.p. 5 b&w.
[First autogiro mail service.]

St. Louis Post-Dispatch

"At the Beaux Arts Ball." *St. Louis Post-Dispatch Pictures*, (St. Louis, Mo.) (Sun., Feb. 4, 1940), p. 8. 10 b&w
[Costume ball in New York City.]

Se (Stockholm)

"Blodfull Brasilianska Far Amerikanarna Att Glömma Kriget." *Se* (Stockholm), [n.d., c.1940], pp. 16-17. 6 b&w, plus 1 b&w on back cover.
[Carmen Miranda. Same essay, abridged and altered, that appeared in the Nov. 1939 *Click.*]

U.S. Camera Annual

1 b&w (Football player George Cafego) on p. 43, plus statement of intent, brief biography on p. 73 of *U.S. Camera, 1941* (1940).

BOOKS

Special Weapon. Published by Business Week Magazine. Printed by Edward Stern & Co., n.p., n.d. [c. 1941], 32 pp.
["Photographs appearing here are from the pages of *Business Week,* and from the following photographers: W. Eugene Smith of Black Star — Underwood & Underwood — Keystone View — INP — Ewing Galloway." Smith photographs on at least pp. 9-20, 22, 23, 26-27. Promotional book for *Business Week* Magazine. 14" x 18", board covers.]

PERIODICALS

American Magazine

"That Wild Johnson Boy," by Gordon Gaskill. *American Magazine,* vol. 131, no. 3 (Mar. 1941), pp. 34-35, 127. 1 b&w.
[Portrait of Howard Johnson drinking champagne with anonymous woman.]

"Interesting People in the American Scene: Sensitive." *American Magazine,* vol. 131, no. 6 (June 1941), p. 79. 1 b&w.
[Safecracker Robert S. Murray.]

"Interesting People in the American Scene: Roughrider." *American Magazine,* vol. 132, no. 1 (July 1941), pp. 78-79. 4 b&w.
[U.S. Army test driver Capt. Eugene Moseley.]

"Interesting People in the American Scene: Confidentially Yours." *American Magazine,* vol. 132, no. 6 (Dec. 1941), pp. 94-95. 1 b&w.
[Group portrait of the Seraphic Secretaries of America.]

Britannica Book of the Year

1 b&w (U.S. Parachute troops training) on p. 67 in: "Armies of the World," p. 64-68. *1941 Britannica Book of the Year.* Encyclopaedia Britannica, Inc., Chicago, Ill., 1941. 748 pp.

1 b&w (Centralia — Salem, Illinois oil field) on p. 530 in: "Petroleum", pp. 529-531. *1941 Britannica Book of the Year.* Encyclopaedia Britannica, Inc., Chicago, Ill., 1941. 748 pp.

Collier's

"Zivic Pride," by Lester J. Biederman. *Collier's,* vol. 107, no. 5 (Feb. 1, 1941), pp. 20, 45. 1 b&w.
[Boxer Fritzie Zivic.]

"Home-Maid Ski Champ," by W.C. Heinz. *Collier's,* vol. 107, no. 9 (Mar. 1, 1941), pp. 22, 44. 1 b&w.
[Skier Marilyn Shaw.]

"Galloping Goons," by Kyle Crichton. *Collier's,* vol. 107, no. 10 (Mar. 8, 1941), pp. 30, 32-33. 2 b&w.
[Notre Dame basketball team.]

"Our New Army: Incidents, Anecdotes and News from Draftee Training Centers." *Collier's,* vol. 107, no. 11 (Mar. 15, 1941), pp. 12, 71. 2 b&w.

"We're in the Army Now," by Lt. Gen. Hugh A. Drum. *Collier's,* vol. 107, no. 12 (Mar. 22, 1941), pp. 15, 60. 1 b&w.
[Portrait of Lt. Gen. Hugh A. Drum.]

"Skeeter Fleet," by Frank D. Morris. *Collier's,* vol. 107, no. 12 (Mar. 22, 1941), pp. 16-17, 55, 56. 1 b&w.
[PT boats.]

"Meet the People," by Robert Andrews. *Collier's*, vol. 107, no. 12 (Mar. 22, 1941), pp. 24-25, 33, 34. 7 b&w.
[Stage musical "Meet the People".]

"Wing Talk: Patricia O'Malley — Press Relations in the Civil Aeronautics Board." *Collier's*, vol. 107, no. 16 (Apr. 19, 1941), pp. 6, 68. 1 b&w.
[Portrait of Patricia O'Malley.]

"Sawdust Doll," by J. Bryan III. *Collier's*, vol. 107, no. 16 (Apr. 19, 1941), pp. 13, 73. 1 color.
[Circus performer Kitty Clark.]

"Paul Vivienne," by Luther Davis and John Cleveland. *Collier's*, vol. 107, no. 17 (Apr. 26, 1941), pp. 21, 81. 1 b&w.
[Actress Vivienne Segal.]

"What Have We Got for Guns?" by Robert McCormick. *Collier's*, vol. 107, no. 18 (May 3, 1941), pp. 14-15, 43. 4 b&w.
[Garand semiautomatic rifle.]

"Bad Bug," by J.D. Ratcliff. *Collier's*, vol. 107, no. 20 (May 17, 1941), pp. 53, 54, 56. 1 b&w.
[Medical researcher Dr. Norman Topping.]

"He Throws Cannonballs," by Arthur J. Daley. *Collier's*, vol. 107, no. 22 (May 31, 1941), pp. 44, 46. 1 b&w.
[Shotputter Al Blozis.]

"Our New Army: Signal Corps." *Collier's*, vol. 107, no. 25 (June 21, 1941), pp. 20-21, 54. 6 b&w.

"Mr. Longfellow and His Boy," by Carl Sandburg. *Collier's*, vol. 107, no. 24 (June 14, 1941), p. 22. 1 b&w.
[Portrait of Carl Sandburg listening to Marianne Lorraine reciting his poetry.]

"Our New Army: Flame Throwers." *Collier's*, vol. 108, no. 7 (Aug. 16, 1941), pp. 14, 32. 2 color.

"Our New Army: Barrage Balloons." *Collier's*, vol. 108, no. 8 (Aug. 23, 1941), pp. 18-19, 26. 5 b&w.

"Monkey-shines," by Kyle Crichton. *Collier's*, vol. 108, no. 10 (Sept. 6, 1941), pp. 16-17, 49. 7 b&w.
[St. Louis Zoo.]

"How to Train a Hunting Dog," by Jim Marshall. *Collier's*, vol. 108, no. 13 (Sept. 27, 1941), pp. 16-17, 60. 9 b&w.

"Go Get'em!" *Collier's*, vol. 108, no. 13 (Sept. 27, 1941), pp. 18-20. 9 color plus color cover.
[Hunting dogs.]

"Our New Army: Army Glider Students." *Collier's*, vol. 108, no. 13 (Sept. 27, 1941), pp. 38-39, 76. 4 b&w.

"Our New Army: Horse Troops." *Collier's*, vol. 108, no. 14 (Oct. 4, 1941), pp. 22-23, 58. 6 b&w.

"The American Miracle," by Walter Davenport. *Collier's*, vol. 108, no. 17 (Oct. 25, 1941), pp. 14-17, 74. 8 color, 3 b&w by Sarra, Smith.
[War production.]

"Fashions with a Future." *Collier's*, vol. 108, no. 21 (Nov. 22, 1941), pp. 19, 54. 2 b&w.
[Fashion designer Mainbocher.]

"Built in a Bathtub," by Frank D. Morris. *Collier's*, vol. 108, no. 24 (Dec. 13, 1941), pp. 20-21, 29. 5 b&w.
[Todd-Bath Shipbuilding Yards in Portland, Maine.]

En Guardia

4 b&w (Newport, R.I. Officers Academy, U.S.S. Constellation, and PT Boats) on pp. 14-15 in: "La Tradicion y el Pensamiento de la Armada." *En Guardia*, (New York, N.Y.) vol. 1, no. 1 (1941).

[Issue devoted to military defense, with strong emphasis on naval might, 8 photographs excerpted from *Life*, etc.]

Life

"Cameraman on Ship Shoots Launching in Reverse." *Life*, vol. 10, no. 2 (Jan. 13, 1941), p. 47. 6 b&w by Smith, 1 b&w by other photographer.
[Launching of merchant ship Rio Parada.]

1 b&w (Portrait of Gen. Hugh S. Johnson) in: "The Ism of Appeasement." *Life*, vol. 10, no. 3 (Jan. 20, 1941), pp. 26-27. 10 b&w by various photographers.

3 b&w (Portraits of Sec. Hull, Sec. Morganthau, Sec. Stimson) on p. 24 in: "Life on the Newsfronts of the World: The Administration's big guns go into action for 'H.R. 1776.' the Lease-Lend Bill." *Life*, vol. 10, no. 4 (Jan. 27, 1941), p. 24. 8 b&w by various photographers.

2 b&w (Army soldiers saluting) on p. 33 in: "These Pictures Show How to Salute." *Life*, vol. 10, no. 4 (Jan. 27, 1941), p. 33. 6 b&w, 4 by Alfred Eisenstaedt, 2 by Smith.

2 b&w (Congressmen in committee) on p. 19 in: "Congressmen Haggle over Lend Lease Bill as New British Ambassador Arrives." *Life,*, vol. 10, no. 5 (Feb. 3, 1941), pp. 17-21. 12 b&w by various photographers.

2 b&w (Civilian defense spotters) on pp. 24, 25 in: "12,000 Civilian Spotters Ward Off Mock Air Invasion of the U.S." *Life*, vol. 10, no. 5 (Feb. 3, 1941), pp. 24, 25. 10 b&w by various photographers.

1 b&w (Carmen Miranda) on p. 50 in: "Movies: South American Movie Stars Invade Hollywood." *Life*, vol. 10, no. 5 (Feb. 3, 1941), pp. 50-52. 11 b&w by various photographers.

"National Defense: Winter at Yaphank." *Life*, vol. 10, no. 7 (Feb. 17, 1941), pp. 72, 74. 7 b&w.
[Camp Upton, Yaphank, Long Island.]

1 b&w (Wendell Wilkie at Lincoln Day Dinner) on p. 31 in: "Wilkie Goes to Bat for Britain and Roosevelt." *Life*, vol. 10, no. 8 (Feb. 24, 1941), pp. 30-31. 10 b&w by various photographers, 1 illus.

1 b&w (Mrs. Abbie Tyler) on p. 46 in: "People. . .," *Life*, vol. 10, no. 11 (Mar. 17, 1941), pp. 45, 46, 48. 8 b&w by various photographers.

3 b&w (Portraits of Francis Verrell and Marvin Grant, Mrs. Leonard Wright, group photograph) on pp. 44, 46 in: "Secret and Official Missions Take Americans Across the Sea to Lisbon." *Life*, vol. 10, no. 12 (Mar. 24, 1941), pp. 43, 44, 46. 12 b&w by various photographers.

1 b&w (Statue of Huey P. Long in Statuary Hall, Capitol Bldg., Washington, D.C.) on p. 33 in: "Life on the Newsfronts of the World: Picture of the Week." *Life*, vol. 10, no. 18 (May 5, 1941).

"Prisons Turn To Sports Programs." *Life*, vol. 10, no. 18 (May 5, 1941), pp. 49-50, 52, 55. 11 b&w.
[Ohio Penitentiary.]

"*Boston Transcript* Folds After 111 Years of Genteel Journalism." *Life*, vol. 10, no. 19 (May 12, 1941), pp. 34-35. 10 b&w.

1 b&w (Tank production plant) on pp. 28-29 in: "Roosevelt Calls For Seven-Day Week as U. S. Defense Machine Begins to Roll." *Life*, vol. 10, no. 19 (May 12, 1941), pp. 27-31. 12 b&w by various photographers.

"Orson Welles." *Life*, vol. 10, no. 21 (May 26, 1941), pp. 108-109. 5 b&w.

"British Sailor Boy Gets His First Look at U.S." *Life*, vol. 10, no. 24 (June 16, 1941), pp. 45-46. 6 b&w, b&w cover.
[British sailor Philip Gamester.]

"Harlem's New 'Congeroo' Gives Girls a Workout." *Life*, vol. 10, no. 24 (June 16, 1941), pp. 49-50. 6 b&w.
[Ann Johnson and Frankie Manning dancing.]

"*Life* Goes Calling at an Officers' Club. Fort Leavenworth Club is One of Army's finest." *Life*, vol. 11, no. 1 (July 7, 1941), pp. 98-101. 2 color by Walter Lane on p. 98; 9 b&w by Smith on pp. 99-101.

2 b&w on pp. 47, 56 in: "The Circus." *Life*, vol. 11, no. 4 (July 28, 1941), pp. 47-56. 20 b&w, 10 color by various photographers.

2 b&w (Young Bob Falkenburg, arm in cast, wins boys [tennis] title) on p. 30 in: "People." *Life*, vol. 11, no. 5 (Aug. 4, 1941), pp. 27-28, 30. 6 b&w by various photographers.

1 b&w (Buster Keaton in *the Gorilla*) on p. 57 in: "Summer Theatre." *Life*, vol. 11, no. 9 (Sept. 1, 1941), p. 53-57, 10 b&w by various photographers.

"Life Goes to a Party. Cafe Socialites splash around in New Yorker's back-yard pool." *Life*, vol. 11, no. 10 (Sept. 8, 1941), p. 108-111. 14 b&w.

1 b&w (Joe DiMaggio) on p. 65 in: "Joe Di Maggio." *Life*, vol. 11, no. 13 (Sept. 29, 1941), pp. 64-67. 4 b&w by various photographers, 1 illus.

"Women's Prisons." *Life*, vol. 11, no. 14 (Oct. 6, 1941), pp. 80-86. 14 b&w.
[New York Westfield State Farm.]

2 b&w on p. 77, 78 in: "Hypnotism is Having New Vogue as Stunt and as Science." *Life*, vol. 11, no. 19 (Nov. 10, 1941), pp. 77-80, 83-86, 89-91. 23 b&w by various photographers.

"Theatre: Cole Porter Tunes and Army Gags Make 'Let's Face It!' A Fun Festival." *Life*, vol. 11, no. 19 (Nov. 10, 1941), pp. 114-116, 119. 14 b&w.

1 b&w on p. 42 in: "John L. Lewis Calls Out Captive Miners." *Life*, vol. 11, no. 19 (Nov. 10, 1941), pp. 42-43. 9 b&w by various photographers.

"'Sons O' Fun' Panics Boston." *Life*, vol. 11, no. 20 (Nov. 17, 1941), pp. 44-45. 10 b&w.

"On Sadie Hawkins Day, North Carolina Coeds Show How to Kiss Girl-Shy Boys." *Life*, vol. 11, no. 21 (Nov. 24, 1941), pp. 40-41. 11 b&w.

"Power Blackout. Southern States Dim Lights as Water Reservoirs Dry Up." *Life*, vol. 11, no. 22 (Dec. 1, 1941), pp. 41, 42, 44, 46, 48. 10 b&w by Smith, 1 by Rudolph Velter on p. 46.

Nations Business

1 b&w (Children laughing) on p. 77 in: "'Dead Beat' Cities Can Reform," by C. A. Crosser. *Nations Business*, vol. 29, no. 7 (July 1941), pp. 72, 74, 76-77. 4 b&w by various photographers.
[Credit: Black Star.]

New York Times

"Sweepswingers," by Lewis B. Funke. *New York Times*, (New York, N.Y.) (Sun., June 15, 1941), Magazine Section 7, pp. 14-15. 9 b&w.
[Credit: W. Eugene Smith - Black Star; sculling shells on the Poughkeepsie River.]

1 b&w (Washington, D.C. National Airport) on p. 3 in: "The American Scene." *New York Times*, (New York, N.Y.) (Sun., July 13, 1941), Rotogravure Picture Section 8, p. 3.

"Mosquito of the Fleet," by George Barrett. *New York Times*, (New York, N.Y.) (Sun., Nov. 9, 1941), Magazine Section 7, p. 16. 1 b&w. Credit: Photograph by W. Eugene Smith, Courtesy of *Collier's* Magazine.
[1 b&w of PT boats.]

P.M.'s Weekly

2 b&w (Children watching play; boy crying) on a single page layout devoted to children in *P.M.'s Weekly* (July 20, 1941). [n.p.]

1 b&w (Harlem Congaroo) on p. 49 in: "Photography: Catching the Eye of Man in Street," [column] by Ralph Steiner. *P.M.'s Weekly*, vol. 2, no. 23 (Nov. 23, 1941), pp. 48-49. 6 b&w by various photographers.
[Smith on p. 49, others by Edward Farber, Ted Moorehead, Clair Harmon, Loren Lansen and Will Connell.]

Popular Photography

Smith listed as prizewinner, mentioned on pp. 18, 126, 130; 1 b&w ("Watchful Waiting") on p. 47; 1 b&w ("Ready") on p. 56 in: "Prize Winners in the Popular Photography 1941 Picture Contest: Black and White."

Popular Photography, vol. 9, no. 6 (Dec. 1941), pp. 18, 40-66, 126-132. 32 b&w by various photographers.
[Smith won the 7th and 15th prizes with these photographs.]

U.S. Camera Annual

2 b&w (Harlem Hop) *U.S. Camera 1942* (1941), pp. 120, 121.

Who

3 b&w (Bert Lahr) on p. 56; (Tobacco Road) and (Betty Hutton) on p. 57 in: "Broadway All Over the Map." *Who*, vol. 1, no. 3 (June 1941). 8 b&w by various photographers. 3 by W. Eugene Smith; 2 by Vandamm; 2 by Carger-Pix; 1 by Aral-Pix.
["Here are some of the shows touring the U.S. this summer . . . ."]

[Probable.] 1 b&w (Sherman Billingsby and Anna Kilsey at table) in: "Inside the Stork Club," by J.P. McEvoy. *Who*, vol. 1, no. 7 (Oct. 1941), pp. 12-15, 61. 1 b&w credited to Black Star.
[New York night club.]

---1942---

BOOKS

Commence Shooting! A Navy Manual on War Photography. Prepared by the Photographic Section, Bureau of Aeronautics, with the collaboration of the editors of *Life* Magazine and of the March of Time Newsreel. Copyright Time, Inc., 1942. 56 pp.
["The photographs in 'Commence Shooting' are from the following sources: Associated Press, Black Star, British Official Photo, European, International News, Life, March of Time, Official U.S. Navy Photo, Pathe News, U.S. Army Signal Corps., Wide

World." Smith pp. 24, 25 (PT Boats); p. 35 (Sailor jumping); possibly p. 27 (Cadets); pp. 42-43 (Building ship).]

PERIODICALS

American Magazine

"Interesting People in the American Scene: Second." *American Magazine*, vol. 133, no. 5 (May 1942), p. 82. 1 b&w.
[Boxing trainer Ray Arcel.]

"Interesting People in the American Scene: Shot Spotter." *American Magazine*, vol. 133, no.6 (June 1942), p. 75. 1 b&w.
[Inventor Sam Berman.]

"Interesting People in the American Scene: Name Caller." *American Magazine*, vol. 133, no. 6 (June 1942), p. 90. 1 b&w.
[Genealogical researcher Edna Casbarian.]

"Interesting People in the American Scene: Jingler." *American Magazine*, vol. 134, no. 3 (Sept. 1942), p. 69. 1 b&w.
[Chairman of U.S. War Labor Board Wm. H. Havis.]

"Interesting People in the American Scene: Maria." *American Magazine*, vol. 134, no. 3 (Sept. 1942), p. 78. 1 b&w.
[Brazilian ambassador's wife, sculptress Mme. deSouza.]

"Interesting People in the American Scene: He Dresses Up the Wacs." *American Magazine*, vol. 134, no. 5 (Nov. 1942), p. 96. 1 b&w.
[Col. Grice, uniform designer.]

Britannica Book of the Year

1 b&w (Closing of *Boston Evening Transcript*) on p. 481 in: "Newspapers and Magazines," pp. 480-483, *1942 Britannica Book of the Year*. Encylopaedia Britannica, Inc., Chicago, 1942. 756 pp.

Collier's

"Kid Sister," by Peter Kalischer. *Collier's*, vol. 109, no.2 (Jan. 10, 1942), pp. 21, 52. 1 b&w.
[Actress Pat Peardon.]

"Good Loser," by Dan Parker. *Collier's*, vol. 109, no. 2 (Jan. 10, 1942), pp. 24, 50. 1 b&w.
[Boxer Freddie Cochrane.]

"Preacher's Daughter," by Kyle Crichton. *Collier's*, vol. 109, no. 6 (Feb. 7, 1942), pp. 20, 37. 1 b&w.
[Author Pearl Buck.]

"Keaney's Couriers," by Kyle Crichton. *Collier's*, vol. 109, no. 9 (Feb. 28, 1942), pp. 17, 24, 25. 1 b&w.
[Rhode Island State basketball team.]

"Sugar Boy," by Stanley Frank. *Collier's*, vol. 109, no. 10 (Mar. 7, 1942), pp. 17, 32, 34. 1 b&w.
[Boxer Sugar Ray Robinson.]

"Our Fighting Men: Floating Armory.". *Collier's*, vol. 109, no. 13 (Mar. 28, 1942), pp. 22-23, 40. 5 b&w.
[U.S.S. Prairie State, naval training ship on Hudson River.]

"The Perils of Judy," by Luther Davis and John Cleveland. *Collier's*, vol. 109, no. 15 (Apr. 11, 1942), pp. 14, 52, 53. 1 b&w.
[Actress Judith Evelyn.]

"Your Sugar Bowl Blows Up," by Frank J. Taylor. *Collier's*, vol. 109, no. 15 (Apr. 11, 1942), pp. 21, 55, 56. 3 b&w.
[Sugar refinery.]

"Hi, Hazel!," by Luther Davis and John Cleveland. *Collier's*, vol. 109, no. 16 (Apr. 18, 1942), pp. 16, 56. 1 b&w.
[Singer Hazel Scott.]

"Our Fighting Men: Medical Corps." *Collier's*, vol. 109, no. 19 (May 9, 1942), pp. 22-23, 62. 5 b&w.
[U.S. Army Medical Corps.]

"Ice Heart," by Grantland Rice. *Collier's*, vol. 109, no. 21 (May 23, 1942), pp. 14, 35. 1 b&w.
[Golfer Ben Hogan.]

"Sky-Scow," by Paul Schubert. *Collier's*, vol. 109, no. 21 (May 23, 1942), pp. 64-65, 67. 2 b&w.
[Navy blimp.]

1 color (Woman in uniform holding flag) on cover of *Collier's*, vol. 109, no. 22 (May 30, 1942).

"Deep in the Heart —," by Quentin Reynolds. *Collier's*, vol. 109, no. 22 (May 30, 1942), pp. 12, 51-53. 1 b&w.
[Paterson, N.J. aircraft plant.]

"Drive Does It," by Craig Wood. *Collier's*, vol. 109, no. 23 (June 6, 1942), pp. 22, 54-56. 3 b&w.
[Golfer Craig Wood.]

"Wing Talk," [column], *Collier's*, vol. 109, no. 25 (June 20, 1942), pp. 8, 52. 1 b&w.
[Airplane turntable, Washington, D.C. airport.]

"That Awful Girl," by Luther Davis and John Cleveland. *Collier's*, vol. 109, no. 25 (June 20, 1942), pp. 17, 40, 41. 1 b&w.
[Actress Mary Andersen.]

"The Old College Try," by Franklin Lewis. *Collier's*, vol. 109, no. 25 (June 20, 1942), pp. 42, 59, 60. 1 b&w.
[Portrait of Cleveland Indians President Alva Bradley, Manager Lou Boudreau.]

"Our Fighting Men: Motor Maintenance." *Collier's*, vol. 109, no. 26 (June 27, 1942), pp. 24-25, 46. 5 b&w.
[U.S. Army Motor Maintenance group.]

"There's Only One Moore," by Stanley Frank. *Collier's*, vol. 110, no. 1 (July 4, 1942), pp. 19-20, 51. 1 b&w.
[St. Louis Cardinals baseball player Terry Moore.]

"No Illusions," by Kyle Crichton. *Collier's*, vol. 110, no. 1 (July 4, 1942), pp. 48, 56. 1 color.
[Broadway producer Cheryl Crawford.]

"Wing Talk," [column]. *Collier's*, vol. 110, no. 4 (July 25, 1942), pp. 8, 32. 1 b&w
[Control tower, Washington, D.C. airport.]

"Lavish Land," by Robert McCormick. *Collier's*, vol. 110, no. 6 (Aug. 8, 1942), pp. 64-66. 8 color.
[Florida Everglades.]

"The Good-Will Kid," by Bob Considine. *Collier's*, vol. 110, no. 10 (Sept. 5, 1942), pp. 54-55. 2 b&w.

"Bobby's Hobby," by Luther Davis and John Cleveland. *Collier's*, vol. 110, no. 11 (Sept. 12, 1942), pp. 19, 24. 1 b&w.
[Comedian Bobby Clark.]

"Game Hunting," by Gurney Williams. *Collier's*, vol. 110, no. 15 (Oct. 10, 1942), pp. 18-19. 5 b&w.
[Photo essay on party games.]

"Riding to Trouble," by Shirley Alexander. *Collier's*, vol. 110, no. 17 (Oct. 24, 1942), pp. 32-33. 3 b&w.
[Ambulance attendants.]

"The Kid from Sunnyside," by Frank Graham. *Collier's*, vol. 110, no. 23 (Dec. 5, 1942), pp. 13, 58. 1 b&w.
[Jockey Basil James.]

"What the Army Drinks," by James W. Wadsworth. *Collier's*, vol. 110, no. 25 (Dec. 19, 1942), pp. 16-17, 96. 5 b&w.
[Survey of U.S. Army drinking patterns.]

"Game Hunting." *Collier's*, vol. 110, no. 25 (Dec. 19, 1942), pp. 94-95. 2 color, 5 b&w.
[Party games.]

En Guardia

[Probable.] 1 b&w (British R.A.F. training planes in Canada) on p. 10 in: "El Arsenal de los E.U.A. Arma al Mundo." *En Guardia* (New York, N.Y.) vol. 1, no. 4 (1942), pp. 10-11. 5 b&w by various photographers.
[Not credited. Very similar photograph in W. Eugene Smith Archives.]

[Probable.] "Paracaidistas — Sorpresa Militar." *En Guardia* (New York, N.Y.) vol. 1, no. 4 (1942), pp. 12-15. 10 b&w.
[Article on parachute training. The lead photograph is by W. Eugene Smith; 3 other probable.]

1 b&w (PT boats) on pp. 16-17 in: "Pequeño Pero Temible." *En Guardia* (New York, N.Y.) vol. 1, no. 7 (1942). 1 b&w by Smith, 2 portraits of naval heroes by unknown photographers.

1 b&w (Soldier in rain) on inside back cover of *En Guardia*, (New York, N.Y.) vol. 1, no. 8 (1942).
[Credited to W. E. Smith - Black Star on p. 40.]

1 b&w (Ships in harbor at night) on pp. 20-21 in: "Bunques-Bunques-Bunques." *En Guardia*, (New York, N.Y.) vol. 1, no. 10 (1942).

Harper's Bazaar

"Junior Officer on a U.S. Battleship." *Harper's Bazaar*, no. 2763, 75th year, (Mar. 15, 1942), pp. 56-57. 6 b&w.

Illustrated (London)

"White House Child." *Illustrated*, [vol. 4, no. ?] (June 20, 1942), pp. 14-15. 5 b&w.
[Same as the Mar. 29, 1942, *Parade* essay.]

Life

"Aides Relieve Nurse Shortage." *Life*, vol. 12, no. 1 (Jan. 5, 1942), pp. 32-34. 11 b&w by various photographers, 7 by Smith.

"Washington Goes To War," by Milton Mayer. *Life*, vol. 12, no. 1 (Jan. 5, 1942), pp. 56-64. 8 b&w by various photographers, 4 b&w by Smith on pp. 58, 59, 60.

"The Ballet." *Life*, vol. 12, no. 3 (Jan. 19, 1942), pp. 44-46. 2 b&w of ballet 'Bluebeard' by Smith on p. 44, 3 color by Gjon Mili.

"Broadway Season. It is full of youth and surprise." *Life*, vol. 12, no. 8 (Feb. 23, 1942), pp. 56-65. 3 b&w of 'Angel Street' on p. 56, 2 color of 'Angel Street' on p. 57, and 11 b&w of 'MacBeth' on pp. 59-61 by Smith; 8 b&w and 6 color by Dmitri Kessel, Eliot Elisofon and Karger-Pix.

1 b&w (Francis Biddle) on p. 107 in story "The Roosevelt Party." *Life*, vol. 13, no. 17 (Oct. 26, 1942), pp. 103-113. 43 b&w by Thomas McAvoy, Myron H. Davis, M. Bourke-White, et al.

Nations Business

1 b&w (Kearny, N.J. Shipyard) on p. 46 in: "A Bridge of Ships," by R. L. Van Boskirk. *Nations Business*, vol. 30, no. 2 (Feb., 1942), pp. 45-46, 58, 60. 1 b&w credited to Partidge, Black Star; 1 b&w not credited.
[Non-credited photograph by Smith.]

New York Herald Tribune. This Week.

"Then They Got Mad," by Arthur Bartlett. *New York Herald Tribune. This Week*, (New York, N.Y.), (Sun., Aug. 12, 1942), Sect. 10 pp. 5-6. 5 b&w.
[Ship construction yard. Credit: W. Eugene Smith.]

Parade

"Soldier's Cop." *Parade*, vol. 1, no. 36 (Mar. 15, 1942), pp. 2-6. 20 b&w plus 1 b&w on cover.
[Army MP John J. Kennedy.]
Also in *Parade's Weekly*, vol. 1, no. 3 (June 6, 1942), pp. 23-28. 21 b&w.

"Symphony in Shirtsleeves." *Parade*, vol. 1, no. 36 (Mar. 15, 1942), pp. 10-11. 15 b&w.
[Sir Thomas Beecham, N.Y. Symphony at Carnegie Hall.]

"Spring Fashions." *Parade*, vol. 1, no. 37 (Mar. 22, 1942), pp. 11-13. 9 b&w.

"Child of the White House." *Parade*, vol. 1, no. 38 (Mar. 29, 1942), pp. 24-27. 9 b&w.
[Diana Hopkins, daughter of Land Lease administrator Harry Hopkins.]
Also in *Parade's Weekly*, vol. 1, no. 1 (May 23, 1942), p. 7. 8 b&w.

"A Sailor in the Making at an Inland Navy Base." *Parade*, vol. 1, no. 40 (Apr. 12, 1942), pp. 2-6. 18 b&w, plus 1 b&w on cover.
Also in *Parade's Weekly*, vol. 1, no. 1 (May 23, 1942), pp. 2-6.

[Possible.] "Shot Put King." *Parade*, vol. 1, no. 45 (May 17, 1942), pp. 18-19. 5 b&w.
[Story of Al Blozis at Georgetown Univ., Smith published a portrait of Blozis in the May 31, 1941 issue of *Collier's*.]

"Miami Beach Air College." *Parade*, vol. 1, no. 45 (May 17, 1942), pp. 21-23. 9 b&w.

"Two Job Governor." *Parade*, vol. 1, no. 47 (May 31, 1942), pp. 11-13. 6 b&w.
[Gov. Blood of New Hampshire — governor and doctor.]

"From Pitcher's Box to Navy Base." *Parade*, vol. 1, no. 48 (June 7, 1942), pp. 12-14. 11 b&w.
[Baseball pitcher Bob Feller.]

"Will the Farmer Win the War?," by Frank De Blois. *Parade*, vol. 1, no. 49 (June 14, 1942), pp. 2-7. 17 b&w, 1 b&w cover.
Also in *Parade's Weekly*, vol. 1, no. 5 (June 20, 1942), pp. 2-7. 17 b&w, 1 b&w on cover.

"Training American 'Commandos'," by Allan Sloane. *Parade*, vol. 1, no. 52 (July 5, 1942), pp. 26-31. 20 b&w.
Also in *Parade's Weekly*, vol. 1, no. 8 (July 11, 1942), pp. 2-7. 20 b&w.

"The Odyssey of a Free Norwegian," by Helge Holt. *Parade*, vol. 2, no. 1 (July 12, 1942), pp. 2-7. 15 b&w, 1 illus., 1 b&w on cover.
[Norwegian ex-patriot training to fly in Canada.]
Also in *Parade's Weekly*, vol. 1, no. 9 (July 18, 1942), pp. 2-7. 15 b&w.

"These Pictures Show What Happens When a U.S. Soldier is Hurt in Battle," by James B. Golden. *Parade*, vol. 2, no. 3 (July 26, 1942), pp. 12-15. 12 b&w.
[U.S. Army Medical Corps.]
Also in *Parade's Weekly*, vol. 1, no. 11 (Aug. 1, 1942), pp. 12-15. 12 b&w.

"The Sky over Corpus Christi is the World's Biggest Classroom." *Parade*, vol. 2, no. 6 (Aug. 16, 1942), pp. 2-7. 14 b&w, 1 b&w on cover.
[Corpus Christi naval air base.]
Also in *Parade's Weekly*, vol. 1, no. 14 (Aug. 22, 1942), pp. 16-21. 14 b&w.

1 b&w "Navy Bomb." *Parade*, vol. 2, no. 6 (Aug. 16, 1942), p. 14. 1 b&w on cover.
Also in *Parade's Weekly*, vol. 1, no. 18 (Sept. 19, 1942), p. 14. 1 b&w.

"Washington Correspondent." *Parade*, vol. 2, no. 9 (Sept. 6, 1942), pp. 2-5. 15 b&w, 1 b&w on cover.
[Harold O. Thompson.]
Also in *Parade's Weekly*, vol. 1, no. 17 (Sept. 12, 1942), pp. 2-5. 15 b&w.

"Portrait of a Top Sergeant." *Parade*, vol. 2, no. 10 (Sept. 13, 1942), pp. 2-5. 9 b&w, 1 b&w on cover.
[First Sergeant James I. Crenshaw at Fort Devens, Mass. This essay includes the photograph in which Smith dressed up as a sergeant and blew himself up with planted dynamite charges.]
Also in *Parade's Weekly*, vol. 1, no. 18 (Sept. 19, 1942), pp. 20-23. 9 b&w.

"Love Story Editor." *Parade*, vol. 2, no. 12 (Sept. 27, 1942), pp. 2-5. 13 b&w.
[Daisy Bacon, editor of *Love Story* magazine.]
Also in *Parade's Weekly*, vol. 1, no. 20 (Oct. 8, 1942), pp. 8-11. 13 b&w.

[Possible.] "Fall Sweaters." *Parade*, vol. 2, no. 12 (Sept. 27, 1942), pp. 19-21. 6 b&w, 1 b&w on cover.
Also in *Parade's Weekly*, vol. 1, no. 20 (Oct. 8, 1942), pp. 19-21. 6 b&w.
[In W. Eugene Smith Archive.]

"Aztec Dream Dance." *Parade*, vol. 2, no. 15 (Oct. 18, 1942), pp. 19-21. 8 b&w.
[Dancer Sondra Barrett.]
Also in *Parade's Weekly*, vol. 1, no. 23 (Oct. 29, 1942), pp. 19-21. 8 b&w.

[Probable.] 1 b&w ("Fighting with Chemistry": Woman scientist holding test tube) on front cover of *Parade's Weekly*, vol. 1, no. 24 (Nov. 5, 1942).
[In W. Eugene Smith Archive.]
Also on cover of *Parade*, vol. 3, no. 26 (Jan. 2, 1944).

"John Doe Came to a Strange Town . . . this is how he made friends." *Parade*, vol. 2, no. 21 (Nov. 29, 1942), pp. 2-5. 12 b&w.
[Defense worker integrating into new community.]
Also in *Parade's Weekly*, vol. 1, no. 29 (Dec. 10, 1942), pp. 2-5. 12 b&w.

"Task Force on Action." *Parade*, vol. 2, no. 23 (Dec. 13, 1942), pp. 3-7. 12 b&w, 1 b&w on cover.

[Staged performance by the "War Department's Army War Show".]
Also in *Parade's Weekly*, vol. 1, no. 31 (Dec. 24, 1942), pp. 3-7, 12 b&w.

"Union Station." *Parade*, vol. 2, no. 23 (Dec. 13, 1942), pp. 26-29. 10 b&w.
[Union Station, Washington, D.C.]
Also in *Parade's Weekly*, vol. 1, no. 31 (Dec. 24, 1942), pp. 26-29. 10 b&w.

[Probable.] "The Miracle of the Sulfa Drug." *Parade*, vol. 2, no. 24 (Dec. 20, 1942), pp. 16-21. 14 b&w.

Popular Photography

1 b&w ("8 o'clock Shadow"; British refugee children) on p. 34 in: "Salon Section." *Popular Photography*, vol. 10, no. 5 (May 1942), pp. 33-34. 19 b&w by various photographers. Technical notes on p. 62.

1 portrait of Smith with caption accepting award on p. 16 in: "Candid Shots," by Andrew B. Hecht. *Popular Photography*, vol. 11, no. 6 (Dec. 1942).
[Smith winning first Prize in *Popular Photography* contest.]

Smith mentioned winning first prize on p. 34; 1 b&w ("Advance Patrol") on pp. 44-45 in: "Prize Winners in the Popular Photography 1942 Picture Contest." *Popular Photography*, vol. 11, no. 6 (Dec. 1942), pp. 34, 44-94, 194. 59 plus b&w by various photographers.

—————————1943—————————

EXHIBITION CATALOGS

The Artist Members of the Independent Voters Committee of the Arts and Sciences for Roosevelt present a *Tribute to President Roosevelt Exhibition* of painting, sculpture, photography and graphic arts.
[Oct. 20-Nov. 7, 1943.] Fine Arts Building, Vanderbilt Gallery, 215 W. 57th St., N.Y., N.Y.
[Checklist of Exhibition: Smith is listed as one of 28 photographers.]

PERIODICALS

American Magazine

"Interesting People in the American Scene: Amazons of Aberdeen." *American Magazine*, vol. 135, no. 1 (Jan. 1943), pp. 98-99. 5 b&w.
[Women defense workers at Aberdeen, Md.]

"Interesting People in the American Scene: American Aces." *American Magazine*, vol. 135, no. 2 (Feb. 1943), p. 114. 1 b&w.
[Male defense workers in Montclair, N.J.]

"Interesting People in the American Scene: Interpreter for the World." *American Magazine*, vol. 135, no. 3 (Mar. 1943), p. 122.
[Linguist Dr. Mario A. Pei.]

"Interesting People in the American Scene: He Puts His Friends to Sleep." *American Magazine*, vol. 135, no. 6 (June 1943), p. 107. 1 b&w.
[Radio announcer Max Mann.]

"Interesting People in the American Scene: He Knows What You're Good For." *American Magazine*, vol. 136, no. 3 (Sept. 1943), p. 128. 1 b&w.
[Aptitude tester Johnson O'Connor.]

"Interesting People in the American Scene: Right Under Hitler's Nose." *American Magazine*, vol. 136, no. 4 (Oct. 1943), p. 130. 1 b&w.
[Office of War Information director of overseas publications John Hackett.]

"Interesting People in the American Scene: Hands that Rock the Cradle." *American Magazine*, vol. 136, no. 4 (Oct. 1943), p. 132. 1 b&w.
[Housewife, mother Gerry Braun.]

1 b&w (PT boat) on pp. 46-47 in: "Night Patrol," by Gordon Gaskill, by courier from North Africa. *American Magazine*, vol. 136, no. 6 (Dec. 1943), pp. 46-47, 121.
[One uncredited Smith photograph of PT boat used as illustration to Gaskill's story.]

Collier's

"Canine Corps," by Avery Stakosch. *Collier's*, vol. 111, no. 1 (Jan. 2, 1943), pp. 32-33. 4 b&w.
[U.S. Army Canine Corps.]

"Food to Fly On," by Hannah Lees. *Collier's*, vol. 111, no. 12 (Mar. 20, 1943), pp. 13, 74. 2 b&w.
[RCAF cooking school.]

"The Voice of Courage," by Kyle Crichton. *Collier's*, vol. 111, no. 12 (Mar. 20, 1943), pp. 30-31, 59. 1 b&w.
[Opera singer Marjorie Lawrence.]

"From the Cradle to the Grave," by George Creel. *Collier's*, vol. 111, no. 15 (Apr. 10, 1943), pp. 12-13, 40. 1 b&w.
[One portrait of elderly man and woman; article about social security.]

"There's Your Horsepower," by W.B. Courtney. *Collier's*, vol. 111, no. 18 (May 1, 1943), pp. 14, 15, 65. Two color by "Fenn Pix and W. Eugene Smith."
[Airplane engines being manufactured.]

"Nijinsky in Jive," by Dorothy Kilgallen. *Collier's*, vol. 111, no. 18 (May 1, 1943), pp. 24, 59. 2 color.
[Dancer Jack Cole.]

"Marriage Under the Microscope," by Gretta Palmer. *Collier's*, vol. 111, no. 20 (May 15, 1943), pp. 12, 74. 1 b&w.
[Portrait of couple.]

"They're Dreaming of Bright Skyways," by W.B. Courtney. *Collier's*, vol. 111, no. 25 (June 19, 1943), pp. 16-17, 70. 1 b&w by Smith, 3 b&w by George DeZayas.
[Four portraits of officials in airplane industry.]

"The Telltale Eye," by Hannah Lees. *Collier's*, vol. 112, no. 2 (July 10, 1943), pp. 21, 61. 1 b&w, 2 b&w microphotos.
[Eye research.]

1 color (Man forging propellers) on cover; commentary on the making of the cover on p. 68 in: "This Week's Work." *Collier's*, vol. 112, no. 8 (Aug. 21, 1943), p. 68.

"A Doctor for All of Us," by James Rorty. Photographed for *Collier's*, by W. Eugene Smith. *Collier's*, vol. 112, no. 8 (Aug. 21, 1943), pp. 29, 53, 54. 2 b&w.
[Nurse-aide Lotta Chaikin.]

"Eve Curie," by Amy Porter. *Collier's*, vol. 112, no. 13 (Sept. 25, 1943), pp. 24, 87, 89. 1 b&w.
[Celebrity Eve Curie.]

En Guardia

"Médico de Aldea. Sus Obligaciones Se Han Multiplicado Con la Guerra." *En Guardia*, (New York, N.Y.) vol. 3, no. 2 (1943), pp. 24-25. 7 b&w.
[Photographs taken from "The Small Town Doctor at War" essay in *Parade* July 4, 1943.]

Illustrated (London)

"Sunday with Wilkie." *Illustrated*, [vol. 5, no. ?] (Apr. 10, 1943), pp. 8-9. 6 b&w.
[From series in *Parade*, Jan. 17, 1943.]

Life

1 b&w from play "Let's Face It" on p. 82 in: "London Theatre. It owes its successful season to six Broadway importations." *Life*, vol. 15, no. 5 (Aug. 2, 1943), pp. 82, 85. 12 b&w by various photographers.

1 b&w (Col. G. Burling Jarret) in: "Letters to the Editors." *Life*, vol. 15, no. 7 (Aug. 16, 1943), p. 6.

New York Herald Tribune. This Week.

"Gun Molls-1943," by Peggy McEvoy. *New York Herald Tribune. This Week.* (New York, N.Y.) (Sun., Feb. 7, 1943), Sect. 9, pp. 12-13. 4 b&w.
[Credit: International. Women testing armaments at the Aberdeen Proving Grounds.]

Parade

"Sunday at Home with Wendell Wilkie." *Parade*, vol. 2, no. 28 (Jan. 17, 1943), pp. 2-5. 9 b&w.

"Betty Watson is a Wave," by Tess Buxton. *Parade*, vol. 2, no. 29 (Jan. 24, 1943), pp. 2-7. 15 b&w.

"He Sets the Tune for the Army." *Parade*, vol. 2, no. 31 (Feb. 7, 1943), pp. 11-13. 5 b&w by Smith on p. 13.
[Undersecretary of War Patterson.]

"The Captain Never Sleeps," by Joseph B. Breed, 3rd. *Parade*, vol. 2, no. 34 (Feb. 28, 1943), pp. 2-7. 12 b&w, 1 b&w on cover.
[Unnamed captain of a naval destroyer.]

"Wings to Speed Industry." *Parade*, vol. 2, no. 35 (Mar. 7, 1943), pp. 12-15. 14 b&w.

"Story of a Song — This is the Army, Mister Jones." *Parade*, vol. 2, no. 35 (Mar. 7, 1943), pp. 18-21. 10 b&w.
[Hit song scenes visualized.]

[Possible.] "America's Narrow Escape." *Parade*, vol. 2, no. 36 (Mar. 14, 1943), pp. 2-7. 11 b&w, 9 b&w portraits.
[Nazi Party in U.S.]

"How a War Worker Spends His Weekly Pay Check," by James B. Golden. *Parade*, vol. 2, no. 43 (May 2, 1943), pp. 2-7. 15 b&w.
[Machinist George Reich.]

"13-Year-Old Veteran." *Parade*, vol. 3, no. 12 (Sept. 26, 1943), pp. 2, 4-7. 13 b&w, 1 b&w on cover.
[Jackie MacInness of Medford, Mass. ran away and joined the Navy at age 13.]

"A Letter from 'Holiday Inn'." *Parade*, vol. 3, no. 21 (Nov. 28, 1943), pp. 20-23. 11 b&w.
[U.S. Army corporal Tom Young, wounded and convalescing at Walter Reed Hospital in Washington, D.C.]

"More Babies Than Ever Before Are Being Born in the U.S." *Parade*, vol. 2, no. 50 (June 20, 1943), pp. 2-7.
[1 b&w by Roy Pinney, 10 b&w by Smith.]

"The Small-Town Doctor at War." *Parade*, vol. 2, no. 52 (July 4, 1943), pp. 2-7. 16 b&w.
[Dr. Nathaniel P. Brooks of Croton, N.Y.]

"They Look for Trouble!" *Parade*, vol. 3, no. 3 (July 25, 1943), pp. 2-7. 14 b&w.
[Submarine.]

"Miles High in the Sky, He Dives Planes at Full Speed to Test Their Strength. Then pilots flying into battle know their planes are safe." *Parade*, vol. 3, no. 3 (July 25, 1943), pp. 21-22. 2 b&w.
[Test pilot Boone T. Guyton.]

"Navy Chaplain." *Parade*, vol. 3, no. 9 (Sept. 5, 1943), pp. 25-29. 10 b&w.
[Naval Chaplain Robert Williamson.]

"From the Fields of America to the Halls of Congress . . .," by James B. Golden. *Parade*, vol. 3, no. 11 (Sept. 19, 1943), pp. 2-7. 11 b&w.
[Congressman C.A. Eaton, Republican of New Jersey.]

Popular Photography

"The Kid Who Lives Photography," by Peter Martin, staff photographer for *Parade*. *Popular Photography*, vol. 13, no. 7 (July 1943), pp. 19-22, 90-91. 7 b&w, 2 portraits.
[Smith biography, with high school interests, early career, meeting his wife Carmen. Concentration on his energy and enthusiasm. More specific information, differing slightly in details, but similar in general scope to the earlier article by Roger Monsell. More information about years 1941-1943.]

"Letters to the Editor: W. Eugene Smith, Pro and Con." *Popular Photography*, vol. 13, no. 3 (Sept. 1943), p. 62.
[Letters from Ronald Allen Reilly, Jack A. Campbell, and Nettie L. Smith in response to "The Kid Who Lives Photography," published in July 1943 *Popular Photography*.]

Smith discussed on p. 16 in: "Candid Shots," by John R. Whiting. *Popular Photography*, vol. 13, no. 5 (Nov. 1943).
[A statement discussing Smith as a war correspondent, comparing him to another photographer named Ralph Morse.]

Reader's Digest

"Gun Molls," by Peggy McEvoy. *Reader's Digest*, vol. 42, no. 251 (March 1943), pp. 47-50.
[1 illus. from photograph by Smith. Condensed from *This Week Magazine, New York Herald Tribune*, Feb. 7, 1943. Article on U.S. Army Equipment Proving Grounds, Aberdeen, Md.]

After months of impatient waiting, Smith was finally able to get a war correspondent's classification by working for *Flying* magazine in the Pacific theatre during the latter part of 1943 and first months of 1944. Smith was based on the aircraft carrier U.S.S. Bunker Hill and photographed naval activities and air strikes during this time. Impatient to get closer to the "real war", Smith rejoined the *Life* staff in the spring of 1944 and began his extraordinarily powerful and humane series of combat photographs during the battles on Saipan, Leyte, Iwo Jima and Okinawa.

1944

BOOKS

Fighting Squadron Eighteen. Published at San Francisco, April 1944. 66 pp.
[1 b&w on p. 37; p. 65; possible on p. 66 and others. Most photographs by Navy photographers and are records. The two photographs by Smith convey emotion and are featured for that purpose. Fighter Squadron 18 was on the USS Bunker Hill and was the squadron with which Smith flew his combat missions in 1943-1944.]

4 b&w (Truk Island raid, Tarawa invasion, Tinian Island raid, Japanese freighter being strafed) noncredited photographs with many other photographs from U.S. Navy, U.S. Air Force, etc. in: *Focus on Victory. The Story of Aerial Photography at War.* Fairchild Camera and Instrument Corporation, New York, N.Y. 1944. [66 pp.].

PERIODICALS

American Magazine

"Interesting People: Mr. & Mrs. Liberty." *American Magazine*, vol. 137, no. 1 (Jan. 1944), p. 107. 1 b&w.
[Mr. and Mr. George Palmer, superintendent of the Statue of Liberty, and wife.]

"Interesting People in the American Scene: Celebrities Pay to Hear Themselves Talk." *American Magazine*, vol. 137, no. 5 (May 1944), p. 132. 1 b&w
[Radio recorder Zeke Rabinowitz.]

"Interesting People in the American Scene: Photo Flash from Kansas." *American Magazine*, vol. 138, no. 5 (Nov. 1944), p. 136.
[Photograph of Smith by Peter Martin; brief biography which emphasizes his exploits as commercial photographer.]

"Letters to the Editor: How to Lose Your Teeth," by Marcia L. Drillis. *American Magazine*, vol. 138, no. 6 (Dec. 1944), p. 4.
[Letter asking for copy of photograph originally published in *Parade* magazine in which Smith was injured in an explosion as described on p. 136 in the November, 1944 issue of *American Magazine.* Copy of photograph reproduced on p. 4 in response to the letter.]

En Guardia

1 b&w (Garapán on Saipan, from the air) on pp. 22-23 in: "La Guerra Se Acerca al Japón." *En Guardia*, (New York, N.Y.) vol. 3, no. 11 (1944), pp. 20-23. 8 b&w by various photographers.
[Garapán by Smith, 1 b&w of marines fighting on Saipan on p. 22 possibly by Smith.]

1 b&w (Engebi airfield) on p. 27 in: "Avance Convergente Hacia el Japón." *En Guardia*, (New York, N.Y.) vol. 3, no. 7 (1944), pp. 26-31. 11 b&w by various photographers.
[Credit: Internationel.]

1 b&w (Variant of Saipan marine drinking from canteen) on inside back cover of: *En Guardia*, (New York, N.Y.) vol. 3 no. 12 (1944).

Flying

"Raid on Wake." *Flying*, vol. 34, no. 1 (Jan. 1944), pp. 28-29. 5 b&w.

"Rabaul Raid." *Flying*, vol. 34, no. 2 (Feb. 1944), pp. 28-29. 6 b&w.

"Future Air Traffic Control." *Flying*, vol. 34, no. 2 (Feb. 1944), pp. 72-74. 3 b&w.
[1 b&w of Washington airport by Smith although credited to Civil Aviation Agency (CAA) in this issue of *Flying*.]

1 b&w (From "Rabaul Raid") on p. 30 in: "Hell-Diver." *Flying*, vol. 34, no. 3 (Mar. 1944), pp. 30-31. 7 b&w.

"Air Strategy in the Pacific," by Brig. Gen. Henry J. Reilly, O.R.C. *Flying*, vol. 34, no. 5 (May 1944), pp. 21-23, 102, 104, 108. 2 b&w.
[Tarawa invasion barges, Engebi bombing.]

"A Carrier At Work." *Flying*, vol. 34, no. 5 (May 1944), pp. 30-42. 18 b&w, 1 portrait of Smith.

1 b&w ("Dilberts"), *Flying*, vol. 34, no. 5 (May 1944), p. 74.

1 color on cover of *Flying*, vol. 34, no. 6 (June 1944).

"Pacific Report." *Flying*, vol. 34, no. 6 (June 1944), pp. 52-53, 130, 134, 138. 3 b&w, 1 portrait of Smith.

1 b&w ("Tarawa") on p. 75 in: "Have You Seen?" *Flying*, vol. 34, no. 6 (June 1944).

2 b&w ("Blasted Bettys" and "Eniwetok-Bound") *Flying*, vol. 35, no. 1 (July 1944), pp. 36-37.

2 b&w ("Incendiary bombing in Pacific") on p. 76 in: "Have You Seen?" *Flying*, vol. 34, no. 7 (July 1944).

"How We Beat the Zero," by Lieut. Comdr. E. Scott McCluskey, U.S.N.R. *Flying*, vol. 34, no. 9 (Sept. 1944), pp. 29, 94, 98, 100. 2 b&w.
[Grumman Avengers in flight; 1 b&w by Smith.]

1 b&w ("Skull & Crossbones Corsairs") *Flying*, vol. 34, no. 9 (Sept. 1944), p. 39.

1 color ("A Vought Kingfisher about to be launched . . .") *Flying*, vol. 34, no. 9 (Sept. 1944), p. 66.

"U.S. Naval Aviation at War." [Special Issue] *Flying*, vol. 34, no. 10 (Oct. 1944).
[Entire issue devoted to U.S. Navy and all photographs credited to U.S. Navy. In fact, at least 3 and probably 5 of the photographs are by Smith (on pp. 48, 49, 66, 132, and 180). This is explained by a statement in the article "A Carrier at Work" in the May 1944 *Flying*: "Many of Smith's aerial battle pictures were so good that the Navy ordered them distributed . . . as official Navy photographs."]

Life

1 b&w (Fatal plane crash) in: "Raymond Clapper." *Life*, vol. 16, no. 1 (Mar. 13, 1944), p. 34. 2 b&w.

"Navy Attacks the Islands." *Life*, vol. 16, no. 19 (May 8, 1944), pp. 22-25. 6 b&w plus portrait and brief biography on p. 17.
Also in *Life*, (Overseas Service Edition), vol. 16, no. 19 (May 8, 1944), pp. 8-11. 6 b&w.
[Photographs from Rabaul, Tarawa, Tinian, Eniwetok Atoll. Portrait, brief biography of Smith on p. 4.]

"Movie of the Week: Gaslight." *Life*, vol. 16, no. 21 (May 22, 1944), pp. 75-78. [6 b&w by Smith from the Broadway version of the play "Gaslight"; 6 b&w by M-G-M of the film.]

1 b&w (Jerome Kern and Oscar Hammerstein) on p. 110 in: "Close Up: Oscar Hammerstein II." *Life*, vol. 16, no. 22 (May 29, 1944), pp. 98-100, 102, 104, 107-108, 110. 8 b&w by various photographers.

"Land Fighting on Saipan." *Life*, vol. 17, no. 3 (July, 17, 1944), pp. 24-25. 3 b&w.

"Saipan. Eyewitness Tells of Island Fight," by Robert Sherrod. Photographs for *Life* by Peter Stackpole and W. Eugene Smith. *Life*, vol. 17, no. 9 (Aug. 28, 1944), pp. 75-83. 14 b&w, 1 illus. 3 by Stackpole, 11 by Smith.
[Portrait and brief biography on p. 19.]

"Japanese Civilians on Saipan." *Life*, vol. 17, no. 19 (Nov. 6, 1944), pp. 45-48, 50. 14 b&w.
Also in *Life*, (Overseas Service Edition), vol. 17, no. 19 (Nov. 6, 1944), pp. 19-22. 14 b&w.

2 b&w (Leyte fighting) on pp. 26-27 in: "Decision in the Phillippines." *Life*, vol. 17, no. 20 (Nov. 13, 1944), pp. 25-31. 17 b&w by various photographers.

"Hospital on Leyte." *Life*, vol. 17, no. 26 (Dec. 25, 1944), pp. 13-17. 9 b&w.
[Portrait and brief biography on p. 11.]

New York Daily News [et al]

1 b&w (Leyte Cathedral) in: "Bles‛   .e the Merciful. Leyte Cathedral Becomes a Hospital for Wounded Yankees." *Daily News*, (New York, N.Y.) (Sat., Dec. 23, 1944), [n.p.].
[Credit: Associated Press.]

1 b&w (Leyte Cathedral) in: "Leyte Cathedral Used as Evacuation Hospital, but Religious Services Continue." *New York Herald Tribune*, (New York, N.Y.) (Sat., Dec. 23, 1944) [n.p.].
[Credit: Associated Press.]

1 b&w (Leyte Cathedral) in: *New York Journal American*, (New York, N.Y.) [damaged, ca. (Dec. 23, 1944)], n.p..
[Large reproduction — full newspaper width, plus four paragraph caption: "Gethsemane on Leyte".]

1 b&w (A Cathedral Shelters the Wounded), with caption on p. 2 in: *New York Times*, (New York, N.Y.) (Sat., Dec. 23, 1944).
[Credit: Associated Press. Leyte Cathedral.]

New York Journal American

1 b&w (Carrier evades bomb), Pictorial Review Section, *Journal American*, (New York, N.Y.) [n.d., ca. 1944], [n.p.]
[For "Near Rabaul" Smith is credited and identified as "Eugene Smith, war correspondent and photographer for *Popular Photography* magazine." The Rabaul raid took place late in 1943, but pictures were probably not released until 1944.]

New York Post

"Photography," by John Adam Knight. *New York Post*, (New York, N.Y.) (May 16, 1944), p. 40.
[Review of Smith's early war photographs exhibited at the Museum of Modern Art, N.Y.]

New York World Telegram

"He Yielded Seat to Clapper in Death Plane: Cameraman Snapped Fatal Flight's End; Here for Treatment," by Roger W. Stuart. *New York World Telegram*, (New York,

N.Y.) (May 9, 1944), [n.p.]. 1 b&w of Smith blowing himself up (*Parade* photograph),plus brief biography.

Popular Photography

"Salon Section: Camera on a Carrier. W. Eugene Smith, War Photographer in the South Pacific, Flew 15 Times Against the Japs," by John R. Whiting. *Popular Photography*, vol. 14, no. 6 (June 1944), pp. 40-51, 58-63. 19 b&w, 2 portraits.
[A detailed, thorough, and accurate account of Smith's work as a war correspondent in the South Pacific for Ziff-Davis Publishing Co. (*Flying*, *Radio News*, *Popular Photography*). Smith was primarily based on the carrier U.S.S. Bunker Hill during this period in 1943-1944. This literate, factual article is the best source of information about this period of Smith's career.]

Recognition Journal

1 b&w on cover (Truk Island raid) and 1 b&w (Japanese freighter being strafed), *Recognition Journal*, no. 11 (July 1944). U.S. War and Navy Depts., p. 24,.

Time

1 b&w (Wounded soldier in Leyte cathedral) on p. 13 in: "U.S. at War." *Time*, vol. 44, no. 26 (Dec. 25, 1944).

U.S. Camera

1 b&w (Engebi Island airfield) *U.S. Camera*, vol. 7,no. 3 (Apr. 1944), p. 14.

U.S. Camera Annual

1 b&w (U.S.S. Bunker Hill) on p. 62; 1 b&w (U.S.S. Bunker Hill) on p. 63; 1 b&w (Truk Island) on pp. 65-65; 1 b&w (Tinian Island) on pp. 114-115; 1 b&w [probable] (Saipan grave) on p. 223 in *U.S. Camera Annual 1945* (1944).

Wichita Eagle

"Former Wichita Photographer Finds Battle Safer Than Assignments in United States." *Wichita Eagle*, (Wichita, Kan.), [n.d., ca. 1944]. 1 portrait of Smith as a teenager.
[Notice of exhibition "Pacific Report" at Museum of Modern Art, N.Y. Lists his accidents, injuries, etc. while on assignments in U.S..]

——1945——

BOOKS

1 b&w on p. 6; 1 b&w on pp. 88-89; 1 b&w on p. 93; 1 b&w on pp. 94-95 in : *Iwo Jima. Springboard to Final Victory*, text by Captain Raymond Henri, United States Marines. U.S. Camera Publishing Co., N.Y. 1945. 96 pp.

The U.S.S. Bunker Hill. November 1943-November 1944. The record of a carrier's combat action against the Axis Nations in the Pacific. Published by and for the personnel of the U.S.S. Bunker Hill at Sea 1944. Published under the direction of Captain Marshal R. Green, U.S.N. Commanding, U.S.S. Bunker Hill, edited by Lieutenant Wallace C. Mitchell, U.S.N.R. and Lieutenant Eugene F. Brissie, U.S.N.R. Printed by the Rogers Printing Co., Chicago, Ill. 1945. 272 pp.
["Photographs: Russell Yoder, PhoM 2c, U.S.N.R., and the photographers of the

U.S.S. Bunker Hill under direction of Photographer C. Warren Lanz. All other pictures are U.S. Navy photographs unless otherwise credited." In fact there are non-credited Smith photographs on at least pp. 17, 20-21, 158, 162, 168. There is also a photograph of Smith "War Correspondent W. Eugene Smith, a Bunker Hill favorite, returns from a combat hop with his story in an alert camera" on p. 271 and commentary about Smith's role, on p. 235, in: "A Field Day Among Bunker Hill Correspondents: We Look At Them," pp. 232-236.]

PERIODICALS

En Guardia

1 b&w (Hospital on Leyte) on p. 3 in: "El Sacrificio de Vidas por la Paz Mundial." *En Guardia*, (New York, N.Y.) vol. 4, no. 4 (1945), inside back cover and pp. 1-5. 10 b&w by various photographers.

1 b&w (Okinawa tanks) on p. 34; 1 b&w (Explosion on Iwo Jima) on p. 35 in: "La Decandencia del Poderio Japónes." *En Guardia*, (New York, N.Y.) vol. 4, no. 7 (1945), pp. 32-35. 8 b&w by various photographers.
[Two by Smith; others possible.]

1 b&w (Flame-throwing tanks on Okinawa) on inside front cover and p. 1 in: "Inmenso Poderío Contra El Japón." *En Guardia*, (New York, N.Y.) vol. 4, no. 8 (1945), inside front cover and pp. 1-5. 11 b&w by various photographers.
[There are six other photographs of fighting on Okinawa, of which one is a probable Smith, and two other are possibles.]

Life

"Letters to the Editors: Hospital on Leyte." *Life*, vol. 18, no. 3 (Jan. 5, 1945), p. 2.
[Letters of appreciation by Mrs. James McSweeney, Bassett Jones and Cpl. Paul B. Lowney.]

1 b&w (Gov. Carlos Romulo of Phillippines) on p. 2 in: "Letters to the Editors," *Life*, vol. 18, no. 6 (Feb. 5, 1945).

"Marines Win Bloody, Barren Sands of Iwo." *Life*, vol. 18, no. 11 (Mar. 12, 1945), pp. 34-37. 4 b&w by Smith, 3 b&w by various photographers.
[Portrait plus biography on p. 23.]

"The Battlefield of Iwo. An Ugly Island Becomes a Memorial to American Valor." Photographs by W. Eugene Smith. *Life*, vol. 18, no. 15 (Apr. 9, 1945), pp. 93-101. 12 b&w plus front cover.

"Pacific War. Savage Battles Continue as Europe's Peace Comes." *Life*, vol. 18, no. 20 (May 14, 1945), pp. 96-97. 2 b&w of Okinawa fighting by Smith on p. 96; unknown photographer on p. 97.

"Okinawa. Except for Japs, It is a Very Pleasant Place." *Life*, vol. 18, no. 22 (May 28, 1945), pp. 87-91. 6 b&w by J.R. Eyerman; 5 b&w by Smith.

"Americans Battle for Okinawa: 24 Hours with Infantryman Terry Moore. 'Wonderful' Smith tells about advancing through the mud and getting hit by a mortar fragment," by W. Eugene Smith. *Life*, vol. 18, no. 25 (June 18, 1945), pp. 19-24. 18 b&w by Smith, portrait of wounded Smith on p. 25.

"War Photographers. *Life* salutes its 21 war photographers who worked up in the front lines...." *Life*, vol. 19, no. 19 (Nov. 5, 1945), pp. 97-113. 22 b&w, 21 portraits by various photographers.
[1 b&w (Saipan baby) plus portrait plus brief biography on p. 102.]

Minicam Photography

"Mother Knows Best?" by Herman G. Weinberg. Photographs by Nettie Lee Smith. *Minicam Photography*, vol. 9, no. 1 (Nov. 1945), pp. 62-65, 122, 124. 4 b&w.
[An interview with Nettie Lee Smith, the

mother of the "celebrated staff photographer for *Life*, and one of the three legendary war correspondent Smiths in the Pacific. . .". 'Wonderful' assumed the delightful role of master-of-ceremonies, interlocutor and kibitzer-extraordinaire during the hour's interview that followed." Nettie often worked as general assistant for Eugene on his assignments, and she often developed and printed his negatives before the war: ". . .I must have around 8,000 negatives by now. Gene probably has over 50,000. . .". Includes portrait of Smith, plus portrait of Nettie Smith by W. Eugene Smith.]

New York Daily Mirror (et al)

1 b&w ("Yanks Burn Japs Out of Holes in Okinawa Hills") *Daily Mirror*, (New York, N.Y.) (Mon., May 7, 1945), p. 13.
[Flame-throwing tanks.]

1 b&w ("American Armor Gains Ground in Hard Struggle for Okinawa") *Daily Mirror*, (New York, N.Y.) (Mon., May 7, 1945), p. 14.
[View of smoke in background.]

2 b&w ("Trail Blazers. Yanks Make It Hot for Nips on Okinawa") *Daily News*, (New York, N.Y.), [ca. May 7, 1945]. Credit: Associated Press. p. 16.
[Medic and soldiers, flame-throwing tanks.]

"Shell Hits Photographer." *New York Herald Tribune*, (New York, N.Y.) (May 25, 1945), p. 7.

"24 Hours with an American Soldier Fighting on Okinawa." *New York Journal American*, (New York, N.Y.) (Fri., June 15, 1945), p. 9. 15 b&w from Terry Moore series, plus statement of Smith's wounding, portrait of Smith in bandages.

"Tales of the Three Smiths Growing. Pack-Rat, Wonderful, and Horrible Smith Have Become Legends in the Pacific," by Malcolm Johnson. *New York Sun*, (New York, N.Y.) (Mon., Apr. 16, 1945), p. 11.
[Harold (Pack Rat) Smith, correspondent for *Chicago Tribune*; W. Eugene (Wonderful) Smith, photographer for *Life*; Irving (Horrible) Smith, movie photographer.]

3 b&w on p. 8, Section C in: "As the Americans Moved In to Attack the Japanese Positions on Okinawa" *New York Times*, (New York, N.Y.) (Mon., May 7, 1945). Credit: Associated Press.
[3 officers; medic & wounded; flame-throwing tanks.]

"U.S. Photographer Wounded on Okinawa." *New York Times*, (New York, N.Y.) (Fri., May 25, 1945), Section 1, p. 3.

"What Do They Do in the Infantry? Here's What They Do on Okinawa." *New York World Telegram*, (New York, N.Y.) (Fri., June 15, 1945), p. 14. 8 b&w from Terry Moore series. All credited to either Acme Newspictures or the Associated Press Photo.

Picture Post (London)

"Will the Japanese Commit Mass Suicide?" *Picture Post*, (London) vol. 26, no. 5 (Feb. 3, 1945), pp. 9-12. 11 b&w.
[From *Life* article 'Saipan'.]

"Hospital in a Cathedral." *Picture Post*, (London) vol. 26, no. 9 (Mar. 3, 1945), p. 10. 4 b&w.
[From *Life* article 'Hospital on Leyte'.]

Popular Photography

1 color (Singer Hazel Scott) on cover of *Popular Photography*, vol. 17, no. 5 (Nov. 1945). Information and b&w reproduction on p. 116.

Saturday Evening Post

Smith mentioned on p. 42 in: "The Correspondents and Their Curly Mustaches," by William L. Worden. *Saturday Evening Post*, vol. 217, no. 32 (Feb. 3, 1945), pp. 14-15, 42, 45. 5 illus., none of Smith.
[W. "Wonderful" Eugene Smith, Harold "Pack Rat" Smith, and Irving "Horrible" Smith mentioned as three war correspondents in the Pacific theatre.]

Stars and Stripes (Pacific Edition)

"Photog Shows Courage He Sought With Camera," by Pfc. Marshall K. McClelland. *The Stars and Stripes*, (Pacific Edition, Honolulu) (May 26, 1945), p. 3.
[Report of Smith's wounding on Okinawa, praise for Smith.]

Time

"A Letter from the Publisher," by P.I. Prentice. *Time*, vol. 46, no. 1 (July 2, 1945), p. 11. 1 portrait.
[Reprints portions of a letter from Smith to Shelley Mydans the night before he was wounded on Okinawa, plus statement from General A.V. Arnold, and commentary by Prentice.]

U.S. Camera

"Wonderful Smith," by Tom Maloney and Paige Abbott. *U.S. Camera*, vol. 8, no. 6 (Aug. 1945), pp. 11-13, 46. 9 b&w combat photos plus portrait.

["A tribute to Eugene Smith, a gallant photographer wounded in action..." by Tom Maloney, with a letter from Paige Abbott to Smith's family describing Smith's wounding, plus excerpts from letters and cables that Smith had written to his wife before the wounding.]

1 portrait, brief biography on p. 36 in: "Correspondents Gallery." *U.S. Camera*, vol. 8, no. 6 (Aug. 1945) pp. 36-37.
[Portraits and biographies of 19 war correspondents.].

1 b&w (Okinawa) on p. 16; 1 b&w (Iwo Jima) on p. 17 in: "U.S. Camera Annual Pays Tribute to the Unsung Heroes in its Victory Issue." *U.S. Camera*, vol. 8, no. 8 (Nov. 1945), pp. 13-17, 47. 19 b&w by various photographers.

U.S. Camera Annual

2 b&w on pp. 70-71 "Asia's Children" (Saipan); 1 b&w on pp. 180-181 "Demolition Charge" (Iwo); 1 b&w on pp. 188-189 "Airbase on Iwo"; 1 b&w on p. 256 "One Out of Five" (Okinawa wounded); 1 b&w on p. 257 "Firing the Crags" (Okinawa); 1 b&w on pp. 260-261 "7th Army Division, Okinawa" (wounded soldier) with long, descriptive paragraph signed W.E. Smith, in: *U.S. Camera 1946* (Victory Volume). (1945).

"Wonderful Smith," by Tom Maloney. *U.S. Camera 1946* (Victory Volume), (1945), p. 372.
[2 b&w by Smith, pp. 371, 372-373].

Smith returned from World War II a wounded hero with a mature and powerful body of photographic work. This work was recognized as a deeply humanistic anti-war statement and it set the stance of his subsequent career. In the late 1940s, shared interests brought him to the New York Photo League. This interest is reflected in the number of references from the League's journal (*Photo Notes*) from 1947 to 1949. Smith also reluctantly continued his connection with *Life* and he remained a staff photographer for that magazine until 1954. During these years a developing series of photo essays displayed his evolution as an artist and, in turn, helped redefine the expressive potential of that form. While the subject matter of these essays varied widely, one theme that persists is Smith's interest in the theatre. Smith also excelled in portraying modern industrial technology and individuals committed to forms of social service. The stronger stories from *Life* include "Folk Singers" (1947), "Country Doctor" (1948), "Hard Times on Broadway" (1949), "Life Without Germs" (1949), "Taft and Ohio" (1949), "Recording Artists" (1951), "Spanish Village" (1951), "A Play for Churches" (1951), "Nurse Midwife" (1951), "Chaplin at Work" (1952), "The Reign of Chemistry" (1953), "My Daughter Juanita" (1953) and "A Man of Mercy" (1954). This period also displays the first hesitant growth of a body of critical literature attempting to deal with Smith as an artist. For the most part, these criticisms are more adulatory than measured.

———1946———

BOOKS

1 b&w (Marine drinking from canteen) on p. 33; 1 b&w (Bert Lahr in "DuBerry Was a Lady") on p. 43; 1 b&w (Dancer) on p. 47; 1 b&w (Wendell Wilkie) on p. 54; 1 b&w (Water toboggan) on p. 56; 1 b&w (WWII) on p. 60; 1 b&w (Planetarium) on p. 67 in: *Photography is a Language*, by John R. Whiting. Ziff-Davis Publishing Co., Chicago and New York. 1946. 142 pp.

"Chapter VIII. Twenty Interviews: W. Eugene Smith." on pp. 136-137 in: *Photography is a Language*, by John R. Whiting. Ziff-Davis Publishing Co., Chicago and New York. 1946. 142 pp.
[Quotes from Smith about his concerns, intentions in photography].

PERIODICALS

Britannica Book of the Year

1 b&w (Tanks on Okinawa) on p. 811 in: "Warfare, Incendiary." pp. 810-811. *1946 Britannica Book of the Year.* Encyclopaedia Britannica, Inc., Chicago, Ill. 1946. 875 pp.

The Camera

"W. Eugene Smith," by Barbara Green, ARPS. *The Camera*, vol. 68 no. 9 (Sept. 1946), pp. 20-25. 7 b&w plus portrait.

[Essentially an extended review of Smith's post-war exhibition at the Camera Club of New York, this laudatory article discusses Smith's techniques, experiences, and ideas about World War II. "I'm no news photographer. My outlook is entirely different from theirs. It made no difference to me, as a news event, that an island was being taken. What I wanted to bring out were the emotions behind the taking of that island."]

Life

1 b&w (Ethel Merman from 1939 play "DuBarry Was a Lady") on p. 85 in: "Ethel Merman." *Life*, vol. 21, no. 2 (July 8, 1946), pp. 84-88, 90, 92, 95. 13 b&w by various photographers.

"Opera: 'Peter Grimes'. Highly Praised British Opera Has Its U.S. Première in Berkshires." *Life*, vol. 21, no. 9 (Aug. 26, 1946), pp. 43-46. 6 b&w.
[Portrait and biography on p. 19.]

1 cartoon by Charles Pearson reprinted from *Yank* in: "Kidding *Life*. Cartoonists have ribbed it for a decade." *Life*, vol. 21, no. 22 (Nov. 25, 1946), pp. 4, 6, 8, 11, 12.
["War photographers were gently ribbed by Charles Pearson in *Yank* during Philippines campaign. Struggling cameraman in foreground is Life's photographer W. Eugene Smith, who was later badly wounded on Okinawa."]

PM

"Hats Off!" *PM* (Wed., May 1, 1946), p. 23. 1 portrait.
[Notice about Smith's exhibition at the Camera Club, 121 W. 68th St., until May 4. Includes brief biography of Smith's war wounding, and mention of his anti-war stance.]

"He Photographed the Real War," by Selma Robinson. *PM's Sunday Picture News* (May 26, 1946), Magazine Section, pp. 1, 7-15. 8 b&w, 3 portraits.
[Detailed account of Smith's WWII career, well-written and thorough; mixing information of his actions with discussion of his feelings and emotions about those events. "I was after a set of pictures so that when people looked at them they would say, 'This is war' — that the people who were in the war would believe that I had truthfully captured what they had gone through . . . I worked in the framework that war is horrible. I want to carry on what I have tried to do in these pictures. War is a concentrated unit in the world and these things are clearly and cleanly seen. Things like race prejudice, poverty, hatred and bigotry are sprawling things in civilian life, and not so easy to define as in war."]

Photo Notes

Notice of exhibition "War Photos of Eugene Smith" on p. 1 in *Photo Notes* (May 1946).
[N.Y. Camera Club, 121 W. 68th St. until Saturday, May 4.]

Popular Photography

Smith mentioned on p. 142 in: "Photographers Ran the War," by John G. Morris. *Popular Photography*, vol. 18, no. 2 (Feb. 1946), pp. 50-52, 142, 143. 9 b&w by various photographs, portrait of Morris.
[Smith mentioned as unusual example of good war photographer.[

Smith's war exhibition mentioned on p. 32 in: "Candid Shots," by the Editor [John R. Whiting]. *Popular Photography*, vol. 18, no. 6 (June 1946).
[Two-paragraph review of Camera Club exhibition, statement about Smith's increasing strengths as a photographer.]

Smith mentioned as exemplar on p. 126 in: "National High School Salon. A teen-ager's bonanza sponsored by Eastman Kodak Company." *Popular Photography*, vol. 18, no. 6 (June 1946).
[Announcement of this contest begins with the narrative of Smith's high school career to *Life* photographer, used as an example of a successful young photographer.]

South Bend Tribune

1 b&w portrait ("N.D. to Display War Photos") in: "Ex-Student Risks Life to Film Battle," by Pearl E. Hafstrom. *The South Bend Tribune* (South Bend, Ind.) (Fri. Evening, June 14, 1946), pp. [n.p.]. 2 columns plus portrait.
[War exhibition at the Notre Dame Library Building. Brief biography, emphasis on Smith's Notre Dame experience.]

U.S. Camera Annual

1 b&w ("A Walk Through a Paradise Garden") on p. 308 in *U.S. Camera 1947* (1946).

BOOKS

The American Master Photographers: A Confidential Report. Trigon Press, Inc., New York, N.Y. 1947. 16 pp. 4 b&w by various photographers.
[Promotional brochure to establish membership to purchase a quarterly series of "a large size picture book devoted either to the work of an individual photographer or to a special phase or problem of photography." The photographers who lent their names to this venture were: Anton Bruehl, Louise Dahl-Wolfe, Alfred Eisenstaedt, Andreas Feininger, Toni Frissell, Philippe Halsman, Fritz Henle, Hoyningen-Huene, Yousuf Karsh, Martin Munkacsi, John Rawlings, W. Eugene Smith, and Ylla.]

PERIODICALS

Life

2 b&w (Singers Camilla Williams, Guiseppe de Luca) on p. 88 in: "Big Music Week. Concert boom hits all-time peak in New York." *Life*, vol. 22, no. 4 (Jan. 27, 1947), pp. 87-93. 16 b&w by various photographers.

1 b&w (Portrait of Moe Annenberg and son) on p. 118 in: "The Racing Racket," by Earl Brown. *Life*, vol. 22, no. 18 (May 5, 1947), pp. 112-126. 8 b&w by various photographers.

"Folk Singers. Mountain people remember the old American music." *Life*, vol. 23, no. 16 (Oct. 20, 1947), pp. 63-66. 6 b&w plus cover.
[Comment on cover photo on page 29.]

1 b&w (Methodist minister Dr. John R. Mott) on p. 113 in: "The Methodist Church. It's strength lies in its great energy." *Life*, vol. 23, no. 19 (Nov. 10, 1947), pp. 113-128. 29 b&w by various photographers, 10 illus.

1 b&w (Portrait of Mrs. Hamilton Fish Webster, 1939) on p. 108 in: "People." *Life*, vol. 23, no. 19 (Nov. 10, 1947), pp. 107-108, 110. 8 b&w by various photographers.

"Theatre: The Case of the Winslow Boy." *Life*, vol. 23, no. 21 (Nov. 24, 1947), pp. 97-98, 100. 2 b&w by Smith. 6 illus.

1 b&w (Singer Ezio Pinza) on p. 132 in: "Ezio Pinza," by Winthrop Sargeant. *Life*, vol. 23, no. 22 (Dec. 1, 1947), pp. 130-132, 135-136, 138, 141-142, 144. 20 b&w by various photographers.

"Miscellany: New York Lamasery. A new Tibetan temple bewilders Staten Island." *Life*, vol. 23, no. 23 (Dec. 8, 1947), pp. 159-160. 3 b&w.
[Collection of art dealer Madame Jacques Marchais.]

Photo Notes

Smith mentioned on p. 1 in: "Leading Photographers to Open New League Gallery." *Photo Notes*, (July 1947), p. 1.
["40 most important American photographers asked to contribute a print to the Photo League for exhibition. Some of the contributors are Berenice Abbott, Lisette Model, Barbara Morgan, W. Eugene Smith, Edward Steichen, and Paul Strand." This is virtually Smith's first mention in *Photo Notes* as a leading photographer, while the others have been mentioned many times in the past.]

"A Letter." *Photo Notes* (Aug./Sept. 1947), pp. 3-4.
[Non-credited, but by Smith; letter is a statement on the responsibility of the magazine photographer towards his job; also notice that Smith "...will speak on his war experience at the Photo League on Friday, Oct. 10th at 8:30 p.m." p. 1.]

"Gene Smith Meeting," by Jo Chasin. *Photo Notes*, (Nov. 1947), pp. 10-11.
[Review of Smith's Oct. 10th talk at the Photo League.]

"Gene Smith Meeting," by Daniel Eisman. *Photo Notes*, (Nov. 1947), p. 10-11.
[Review of Smith's Oct. 10th talk at the Photo League.]

"Gene Smith Meeting," by Dan Weiner. *Photo Notes*, (Nov. 1947), p. 10.
[Review of Smith's Oct. 10 talk at the Photo League.]

————————1948————————

BOOKS

"W. Eugene Smith on Photo Journalism," pp. 189-196 in: *The Twin-Lens Camera Companion*, by H. S. Newscombe, F.R.P.S., with contributions by Philippe Halsman, Roy Pinney, Ylla, W. Eugene Smith, George Karger, Arnold Eagle, Nelson Morris, Fritz Henle, Andreas Feininger, Fritz Goro. The Focal Press, London, New York. 1948. 320 pp. 4 b&w (World War II) by Smith.

EXHIBITION CATALOGS

1 b&w (Pat and Juanita, variation 13) on p. 14 in *This is The Photo League*. [Exhibition of 1948-1949]. The Photo League, New York, 1948. 24 pp.
[Catalogue of exhibition. W. Eugene Smith was president of the Photo League during this period.]

PERIODICALS

America Illustrated

"Derevenskij Vrac. Prijnatel 'nost' bolnyx - nagrada za bolshoj trud." (Country Doctor. The gradituge of patients - the reward for his hard work). *Amerika Illjustrirovannyj zvurnal* (America Illustrated). [Published by the United States Information Agency for distribution in the Soviet Union. No. 54 (n.d., ca.1948), pp. 3-9. 14 b&w.]
[Essay from Sept. 29, 1948 *Life*.]

Editor & Publisher

"Photography: Smith Carries Torch With His Camera," by James L. Collings. *Editor & Publisher* (Oct. 2, 1948), p. 46. 1 portrait.
[Interview, discussing Smith's methods and ideas about photojournalism, focusing on his handling of the just-published and well-received "Country Doctor" essay. "I'm still searching desperately for the truth, for the answer to how to do a picture story. . . . The majority of photo stories require a certain amount of setting up, re-arranging and stage direction to bring pictorial and editorial coherency to the pictures. . . . If, however, the changes become a perversion of the actuality for the sole purpose of making a more dramatic or salable picture, the photographer has indulged in poetic license that shouldn't be. . . ." [For the "Country Doctor" essay] "I just faded into the wallpaper . . . I insist on doing it my way — just so long as that way is legitimate. . . . Photography is not just a job to me. I'm carrying a torch with a camera, and it won't embarrass me if you say just that."

F.Y.I. (For Your Information)

"An Instinct for Realism." *F.Y.I.* (ca. 1948), p. 3. 1 portrait.
[Brief biography of Smith plus information about "Country Doctor" essay plus portrait by Robert Harrah. *F.Y.I.* was an internal publication of Time-Life.]

Life

2 b&w on p. 113 and p. 127 in: "Tennessee Williams," by Lincoln Barnett. *Life*, vol. 24, no. 7 (Feb. 16, 1948), pp. 118-127. 6 b&w by various photographers.

1 b&w from dance "And Daddy was a Fireman" on p. 79 in: "Fables in Dance: His Father's Career and Thurber's Impressionable Animals give Charles Weidman his Themes." *Life*, vol. 24, no. 16 (Apr. 19, 1948), pp. 79-80, 83, 84. 7 b&w by Lisa Larsen, 1 b&w by Smith.

"Pictures of the Week. Taft and Stassen Get Headquarters Mixed." *Life*, vol 24, no. 18 (May 3, 1948), pp. 32-33. 1 b&w of Robert Taft on p. 32 by Smith. 1 b&w of Stassen by Hank Walker.

"Trial by Jury. Life Reports Case of the State vs. Bowers." Photographs for Life by W. Eugene Smith. *Life*, vol. 24, no. 20 (May 17, 1948), pp. 124-133. 40 b&w.

"Rediscovered Genius. Elie Nadelman's Sculpture Emerges from Two Decades of Obscurity." *Life*, vol. 24, no. 21 (May 24, 1948), pp. 119-120, 122. 3 b&w by Smith, 3 by various photographers.

"Class of '48. Its Members are Going into a World Eager to Give Them Jobs." *Life*, vol. 24, no. 23 (July 7, 1948), pp. 111-119. 20 b&w.

"Rehearsal Throes. Young Hopefuls Sing and Dance to Get Ready for a New Season." *Life*, vol. 25, no. 12 (Sept. 20, 1948), pp. 103-106. 8 b&w, plus cover.

"Country Doctor. His Endless Work Has Its Own Rewards." Photographed for *Life* by W. Eugene Smith. *Life*, vol. 25, no. 12 (Sept. 20, 1948), pp. 115-126. 28 b&w.

1 b&w (Singer Lena Horne) on p. 101 in: "Nightclubs: Lena Horne." *Life*, vol. 25, no. 16 (Oct. 18, 1948), pp. 101-102. 1 b&w by Smith, 5 b&w by various photographers.

"Theatre: 'Edward, My Son'. Robert Morely is Superb as a Father Who Commits Crimes for His Child." *Life*, vol. 25, no. 16 (Oct. 18, 1948), pp. 111-114. 7 b&w.

1 b&w (Composer Heitor Villa-Lobos) on p. 108 in: "Broadway Tries Hard. New Productions Break Away from Old Patterns." *Life*, vol. 25, no. 17 (Oct. 25, 1948), pp. 102-108. 8 b&w by various photographers.

3 b&w (Air Force Generals Muir S. Fairchild, Edwin W. Rawlings, and Curtis E. LeMay) on p. 88 in: "The Air Force's New Command Team." *Life*, vol. 25, no. 18 (Nov. 1, 1948), pp. 87-88, 90. 6 b&w by various photographers.

"Lung is Collapsed by Plastic Balls. New and Controversial Technique is Designed to Immobilize Tuberculous Organ without Disfiguring the Chest." *Life*, vol. 25, no. 18 (Nov. 1, 1948), pp. 127-128. 3 b&w.

"Close up: Joe Gatto, Primitive. An Ex-prize Fighter Solemnly Paints Scenes He Never Saw and Sells Them for Big Money," by Winthrop Sargeant. *Life*, vol. 25, no. 19 (Nov. 8, 1948), pp. 72-80. 3 b&w, 1 b&w illus., 2 color illus.

2 b&w (Harry Truman) on p. 41 and p. 42 in: "Truman Works a Political Miracle." *Life*, vol. 25, no. 20 (Nov. 15, 1948), pp. 37-49. 73 b&w by various photographers.

1 b&w (President Truman), front cover, vol. 25, no. 24 (Nov. 22, 1948), *Life*.

1 b&w (Paul Muni in telecast of Elmer Rice's "Counselor-at-Law") on p. 132 in: "Bigtime Television. New Medium Booms into Maturity with Good Dramas, Well-Known Story." *Life*, vol. 25, no. 23 (Dec. 6, 1948), pp. 131-141. 50 b&w by various photographers.

1 b&w (Monica Dickens) on p. 77 in: "My Great Grandfather Charles Dickens," by Monica Dickens. *Life*, vol. 25, no. 26 (Dec. 27, 1948), pp. 75-78, 81, 82, 84. 1 b&w, 10 illus.

Middle Park Times and Kremmling Record

"Middle Park Hospital To Be Featured in Life Magazine." *The Middle Park Times and Kremmling Record*. (Kremmling, Grand County, Colo.) vol. 68, no. 7 (Thurs., July 22, 1948), pp. 1, 7.
["For nearly a month, W. Eugene Smith and Robert Harrah, both photographers for Life magazine ... have been acompanying Dr. Ernest G. Ceriani of Kremmling. ..."]

The Museum of Modern Art Bulletin

1 b&w (Musicians Bruno Walter and Joseph Szigeti) on p. 6 [Miscredited to Fred Plaut]; 2 b&w (Musicians Charles Munch, Artur Rodzinski) on p. 7 in: "Music and Musicians," [by Edward Steichen], with an appended essay "Beat Me, Daddy, F8 to the Bar!" by Barnett Bildersee, *PM* on p. 7. *The Museum of Modern Art Bulletin*, vol. 15, no. 2 (Jan. 1948), pp. 1, 3-6. 16 b&w by various photographers. [Exhibition "Music and Musicians," Museum of Modern Art, New York, N.Y. Six photographers. Adrian Siegel, Fred Plaut, W. Eugene Smith, Yousuf Karsh, Philippe Halsman and Gjon Mili.]

Photo-Graphic 1949

1 b&w (Rodzinski at recording session) on p. 84; 1 b&w ("Before No Other Will" [Smith's Mother]). *Photo-Graphic 1949*, p. 94. The Annual of America's Leading Photographers. Selected and Edited by the American Society of Magazine Photographers. Designed by Bradbury Thompson. Whittlesey House. McGraw-Hill Book Co., Inc., New York. 1948. 212 pp.

Photo Notes

Smith mentioned on pp. 1, 6, *Photo Notes* [Special number] (Jan.1948), pp. 1-8.
[In response to the Attorney General's list of subversive organizations released Dec. 4, 1947, the Executive Committee of the Photo League held an emergency meeting. Also asked to attend were Beaumont Newhall, Paul Strand and Smith. Further on p. 6: "Having been asked by the Executive Committee to draft his [official letter to Attorney General Clark], Gene Smith reported that he had already discarded two drafts and was working on a third. Every shade of meaning, in his opinion, is important, and we should not act hastily, or our efforts will be wasted."]

Smith mentioned, *Photo Notes*, (Mar. 1948), p. 1.
[Speaker, with Bruce Downes, Sid Grossman, Paul Strand and Beaumont Newhall, in a symposium "Photography As We See It" to be held Friday, March 19.]

Smith mentioned on p. 6 in: "Ansel Adams at the Photo League," by Lester Taikington. *Photo Notes*, (Mar. 1948), pp. 4-6.
[Report on controversial talk given by Adams at Photo League on Nov. 28, 1947. Smith and Philippe Halsman reported to disagree with Adams' distinctions on reportage.]

Smith mentioned as exemplar on p. 9 in: "Reviews: 'Photo Arts' ... A New Publication," by Walter Rosenblum. *Photo Notes*, (Mar. 1948), pp. 8-9.
[Book review: *Photo Arts* magazine. Smith mentioned as example of "... creative work under commercial circumstances in last war ...."]

Smith mentioned as exemplar on p. 11 in: "Reviews: Slightly Out of Focus by Robert Capa," by John Vachon. *Photo Notes*, (Mar. 1948), p. 11.
[Book review: *Slightly Out of Focus* by Robert Capa. "It is not the impassioned indictment of war that Gene Smith's pictures are. But it is an honest and moving story...."]

"Music and Musicians — Exhibit," by Dan Weiner. (Exhibition review: "Music & Musicians", Museum of Modern Art, New York, N.Y.) *Photo Notes*, (Mar. 1948), pp. 11-12.
[Smith participated in this six-person exhibition, discussed in review by Weiner. Other photographers were Yousuf Karsh, Philippe Halsman, Gjon Mili, Adrian Siegel, and Fred Plaut.]

"Photo League Officers for 1948-1949." *Photo Notes* (June 1948), p. 2.
["List of Officers of Photo League for 1948-49, Gene Smith — president; Walter Rosenblum — vice president; Jo Chasin — treasurer;" etc. ...]

"Photographic Journalism," by W. Eugene Smith. *Photo Notes*, (June 1948), pp. 4-5.
[Text of speech that "Smith would have given in the Symposium 'Photography As We See It,' if he had not been grounded in Pittsburgh that evening." "Photography is a potent medium of expression. Properly used it is a great power for betterment and understanding. Misused, it has and will fire much trouble. ... The photographer must bear the responsibility for his work and its effect...."]

Smith mentioned on p. 32 in: "50 Photographs by 50 Photographers," by Dan Weiner. *Photo Notes*, (Fall 1948), pp. 31-33.
[Exhibition review: "50 Photographs by 50 Photographers," Museum of Modern Art, New York, N.Y. The exhibition was a survey of photography from 1845 to 1948. Smith was one of the participants.]

Santa Fe News, et al.

"Letters: Mr. Citizen," by Will Shuster. *Santa Fe New Mexican*, (Santa Fe, N. M.) (Wed., Feb. 25, 1948), p. [n.p.]
[Letter praising Smith's exhibition "currently" at the Santa Fe Art Museum.]

"Art in the News," by Alfred Morang. *Santa Fe News*, (Sante Fe, N. M.), no. 51 [Feb. 1948], p. 2.
[Paragraph notice about the exhibition of photographs by W. Eugene Smith of *Life* magazine ... no dates for show, no locale, no titles given.]

"Eugene Smith Exhibits at Art Gallery." *Unidentified newspaper* (Santa Fe, N.M.), n.d., n.p.
[Announcement of exhibition at the Santa Fe Art Museum — will continue through February. Brief history of Smith's project in New Mexico for *Life* (never published), brief description of show.]

U.S. Camera Annual

1 b&w (Pianist Mary Lou Williams), *U.S. Camera 1949* (1948), p. 178.

EXHIBITION CATALOGS

"The One-Shot Editorial Photograph." W. Eugene Smith interviewed by K. Chester. *The [1st] Exhibition of the American Society of Magazine Photographers Program.* A.S.M.P., New York, N.Y. [1949] [32 pp.], p. 5. 1 b&w plus 1 portrait; plus photographs no. 43 "Portrait of Randall Davey"; no. 52 "Tuckahoe, N.Y. Girl with a song," in program listings. Exhibition consisted of 251 photographs by numerous photographers.

PERIODICALS

Life

"Hard Times on Broadway. Too Many Actors with Too Few Jobs Dream and Scrabble to Keep Sock and Buskin Together." Photographs for *Life* by W. Eugene Smith. *Life*, vol. 26, no. 7 (Feb. 14, 1949), pp. 87-95. 21 b&w.

"Theatre: Death of a Salesman. Fine Tragedy Becomes a Critical and Box-Office Sensation." *Life*, vol. 26, no. 8 (Feb. 21, 1949), pp. 115, 117-118, 121. 8 b&w.

1 b&w (Cornell University campus) on p. 113 in: "Intercollegiate Bull Session," by John McPartland. *Life*, vol. 26, no. 13 (Mar. 28, 1949), pp. 112-114, 116, 118, 121, 124. 6 b&w by various photographers, 1 illus.

"South Pacific. Martin and Pinza Make Theatre History in Musical Play." *Life*, vol. 26, no. 16 (Apr. 18, 1949), pp. 93-96. 10 b&w by Smith, 1 b&w by John Swope.

"Princeton's Bellmaster. A U.S. College Professor is One of the World's Best Carilloneurs." *Life*, vol. 26, no. 18 (May 2, 1949), pp. 125-126, 128. 9 b&w.
[Arthur Bigelow.]

"Germany's Boss. John McCloy Accepts His Hardest Chore: U.S. High Commissioner." *Life*, vol. 26, no. 22 (May 30, 1949), pp. 35, 36. 1 b&w by Smith, 1 b&w by James Whitmore.

"Albert Schweitzer. Reverence for Life and Faith in the Individual Against the Mass are Keys to the Philosophy of a Great Thinker and Humanitarian," by Winthrop Sargeant. *Life*, vol. 27, no. 4 (July 25, 1949), pp. 74-80, 82. 2 b&w by Smith, 3 b&w by various photographers.

"Life Without Germs. Microbe-Free Animals Grow to Maturity and Bear Young within a Strange, Free New Sterile Laboratory at Notre Dame." Photographs for *Life* by W. Eugene Smith. *Life*, vol. 27, no. 13 (Sept. 26, 1949), pp. 107-113. 18 b&w, 1 illus.

"Life Congratulates . . . Charles E. Ives." *Life*, vol. 27, no. 18 (Oct. 31, 1949), p. 45. 1 b&w.

"Theatre: 'Lost in the Stars.' Broadway Season's First Real Hit is a Musical Play Based on the Fine Novel, 'Cry, the Beloved Country.'" *Life*, vol. 27, no. 20 (Nov. 14, 1949), pp. 143-146, 149. 7 b&w by Smith, 2 by various photographers.

"Theatre Girl. Resolute Young Actress Keeps Plugging to Get Her Break on Broadway." Photographed for *Life* by W. Eugene Smith. *Life*, vol. 27, no. 21 (Nov. 21, 1949), pp. 103-109. 20 b&w.
Also in *Life* (International edition), vol. 7, no. 12 (Dec. 10, 1949 [?]), pp. 52-57. 17 b&w.
[Slightly different layout, same images, less three.]

"Taft and Ohio. Mr. Republican Fights for Himself and His Party." *Life*, vol. 27, no. 22 (Nov. 28, 1949), pp. 101-108. 18 b&w.
Also in *Life* (International edition), vol. 7, no. 13 (Dec. 19, 1949), pp. 52-59. 17 b&w. [Same layout, except p. 108 dropped.]

Photo Notes

Smith mentioned on p. 19 in: "The Camera and the Audience," by Louis Clyde Stoumen. *Photo Notes*, (Spring 1949), pp. 18-20.

[Book review: *Photo-Graphic 1949*, the Annual of the American Society of Magazine Photographers.]

U.S. Camera Annual

1 b&w (Child of song) on p. 272 of *U.S. Camera 1950*, (1949).

───────── 1950 ─────────

BOOKS

1 b&w (Saipan bombing) on p. 329; 1 b&w (Saipan fighting) on p. 330; 3 b&w (Saipan) on p. 331; 1 b&w (Leyte Cathedral) on p. 332; 1 b&w (B-29 on Iwo Jima) on p. 340; 1 b&w (Explosion, Iwo Jima) on pp. 340-341; 1 b&w (Okinawa) on p. 348; 3 b&w (Okinawa) on p. 349; 1 b&w (Saipan Marine) on p. 358 in: "Chapter XII: Victory in the Pacific," pp. 321-359. *Life's Picture History of World War II*. Time, Inc., New York, N.Y., 1950. 368 pp.

1 b&w (football player George Cafego) on p. 357 in: *Il Messaggio Dalla Camera Oscura*, di Carlo Mollino. Presso La Casa Editrice Chiantore di Torino. Torino, Italy. 1950. 445 pp.

EXHIBITION CATALOGS

1 b&w (Portrait of musician Charles Muench) on p. 8; brief biography [in German] on p. 19 in: *Scharf und Unscharf Eingestellt. Americanische Fotografen von Heute*. Foreword by Edward Steichen. [In German.]

[An exhibition from the Museum of Modern Art, New York, N.Y.]
Sponsored by Fine Arts Section, Information Centers Branch, HICOG, Frankfurt; and Cultural Institutions, Office of the Land Commissioner for Wuerttemberg-Baden. Printed in Stuttgart, W. Germany. 1950. 20 pp. 10 b&w by various photographers.

PERIODICALS

Life

1 b&w (Gregory Peck in "Twelve O'Clock High") on cover of *Life*, vol. 28, no. 8 (Feb. 20, 1950).

1 b&w (Clement Attlee giving a speech) on p. 31 and 3 b&w ("Welsh Miners," "Welsh cattle," and "Liberal Sidney Protheroe") on p. 34 in: "Britain's Future Is Put Up to Voters." *Life*, vol. 28, no. 8 (Feb. 20, 1950), pp. 29-35. 29 b&w by various photographers.

1 b&w (Clement Attlee) on p. 21; 1 b&w (Election watchers) on p. 22 in: "Attlee Surveys the Ruins of Victory." *Life*, vol. 28, no. 10 (Mar. 6, 1950), pp. 21-23. 9 b&w by various photographers.

1 b&w (Mary Martin and Enzio Pinza in "South Pacific") in: "Theatre: Rogers Has Share in Pulitzer Prize." *Life*, vol. 28, no. 20 (May 15, 1950), pp. 103-104, 106. 14 b&w by various photographers.

U.S. Camera Annual

1 b&w (WWII Marine drinking from canteen), with caption "Again!", on p. 2; 1 b&w (Clement Attlee) on p. 336 of *U.S. Camera 1951*, (1950).

1951

BOOKS

9 b&w (Country Doctor) on pp. 6-7; 4 b&w (Spanish Village) on pp. 20-23; 1 b&w (Clement Attlee) on p. 39; 1 b&w (Leyte Hospital) on p. 107; 1 b&w (Saipan baby) on p. 111; in: *Memorable Life Photographs*. Foreword and comment by Edward Steichen. Museum of Modern Art, New York, N.Y. Time, Inc. 1951. 120 p.

PORTFOLIO

Spanish Villge. Life Magazine. [1951] 8 loose sheets in a printed folder.
[*Life* published, as a publicity bochure, 8 sheets (1 photograph per sheet) that were not included in the "Spanish Village" essay in the April 9, 1951 *Life*. Includes a photograph on the wrap-around cover, with commentary about the difficulties associated with obtaining the essay.]

PERIODICALS

American Photography

"What is Modern Photography? A Symposium at the Museum of Modern Art, Nov. 20, 1950." *American Photography*, vol. 45, no. 3 (Mar. 1951), pp. 146-153.
[A report of the symposium by Walter Rosenblum mentions on pp. 150-151: "The bright spot of the symposium was the impromptu speech of W. Eugene Smith, who spoke during the discussion period. . . . It is commonly agreed by his fellow photographers that Smith represents photojournalism at its best. His own personal honesty is married to the most eloquent photographic perception. . . . 'Life has 24 million readers,' Smith said, 'and I am responsible to each one of them for what I do and for those pictures of mine that are published.' As he spoke, one could feel a spark traveling through the audience, a spark which ignited tremendous applause when the statement was completed. . . ."]

Architectural Forum

1 b&w (Steel worker and blast furnace) on p. 149 in: "Today's Industrial Building: A Blend of Architecture and Engineering, of Plant and Process. Giffels & Vallet, Inc., L. Rossetti have mastered this formula." *Architectural Forum*, vol. 94, no. 9 (May 1951), pp. 144-152. 9 b&w by various photographers.

F. Y. I. (For Your Information)

"Letter from Zagreb." *F. Y. I.* (Dec. 21, 1951), p. 2. 1 b&w (Spanish spinner.)
[Note that Dr. Juraj Korbler of Zagreb, Yugoslavia had written for permission to use the Spanish Spinner photograph in an article on lip cancer. At this time only 50 copies of *Life* were being allowed into Yugoslavia. *F. Y. I.* was an internal publication of Time-Life.]

Life

"Theatre: '20th Century' Gloria Swanson and José Ferrer Make Lark Out of Rowdy Revival." *Life*, vol. 30, no. 8 (Feb. 19, 1951), pp. 117-118, 120. 7 b&w.

"Speaking of Pictures ... Missouri 'U' Names Life's Eisenstaedt Top News Photographer of the Year." *Life*, vol. 30, no. 10 (Mar. 5, 1951), pp. 18-20. 12 b&w by various photographers.
["Best Feature Award" went to W. Eugene Smith's photograph of Welsh Miners (*Life*, Feb. 20, 1950). 1 b&w of Welsh Miners on p. 19.]

"Recording Artists. Great Musicians Perform in a World the Public Never Sees." Photographed for *Life* by W. Eugene Smith. *Life*, vol. 30, no. 13 (Mar. 26, 1951), pp. 122-127. 22 b&w.
Also in *Life* (International edition), vol. 11, no. 9 (Oct. 22, 1951), pp. 50-55. 22 b&w. [Same layout.]

"Spanish Village. It Lives in Ancient Poverty and Faith." Photographed for *Life* by W. Eugene Smith. *Life*, vol. 30, no. 15 (Apr. 9, 1951), pp. 120-129. 17 b&w.

"Theatre: Last Glimpse of 'De Lawd.' The Pastures Become Green Again." *Life*, vol. 30, no. 16 (Apr. 16, 1951), pp. 67-69. 5 b&w.

"Theatre: The King and I. Latest Rogers-Hammerstein Triumph Comes Up with New Star as Monarch Who Met a Schoolmarm." *Life*, vol. 30, no. 17 (Apr. 23, 1951), pp. 79-80, 82, 87. 9 b&w.

3 letters praising Spanish Village in: "Letters to the Editors: Spanish Village." *Life*, vol. 30, no. 18 (Apr. 30, 1951), p. 4.

"Theatre: 'Remains to Be Seen.' Lindsay and Crouse Write a Mystery-Comedy Around a Drum-Playing Hero and a Twice-Killed Corpse." *Life*, vol. 31, no. 16 (Oct. 15, 1951), pp. 169-170, 172, 174. 9 b&w.

"Religion: A Play for Churches. A Religious Drama by Christopher Fry Will Tour the U.S." *Life*, vol. 31, no. 20 (Nov. 12, 1951), pp. 73-75, 77. 8 b&w.
["A Sleep of Prisoners."]

1 b&w (Dennis Stock, First prize winner in Life Young Photographers Contest) *Life*, vol. 31, no. 22 (Nov. 26, 1951). p. 15.
[The ten winners' portraits were presented on p. 15, their photographs on other pages.]

"Nurse Midwife. Maude Callen Eases Pain of Birth, Life and Death." Photographed for *Life* by W. Eugene Smith. *Life*, vol. 31, no. 23 (Dec. 3, 1951), pp. 134-145. 30 b&w.

"Letters to the Editor: 'Nurse Midwife'." *Life*, vol. 31, no. 26 (Dec. 24, 1951), p. 2. 1 portrait of Maude Callen. [12 letters published, editorial statement that $3,689.03 in cash plus other items sent to Maude Callen from readers.]

Modern Photography

"W. Eugene Smith's Spain," by Jacquelyn Judge. *Modern Photography*, vol. 15, no. 12 (Dec. 1951), pp. 78-87, 124. 9 b&w.
[Nine "Spanish Village" photographs powerfully presented (five for the first time) with an introductory text that describes the history of this essay. "Once in Spain, he spent a month and a half, taking few pictures, driving 7,500 miles in search of his story. ... In Deleitosa, for three weeks he photographed with simple tools, eminently suited to his subject matter. ..."]

Mundo Hispánico (Madrid)

"Carta al Editor de 'Life' — Letter to the Editor of 'Life,'" by Gaspar Gomez de la Serna. *Mundo Hispánico* (Madrid), no. 40, 4th Year (July 1951), pp. 17-19.
[Letter in Spanish on pp. 17, 19, English translation on p. 18 responding to the "Spanish Village" essay, protesting that the photographs chosen were an unfair representation of the present Spanish economy.]

News Pictures of the Year

1 b&w (Welsh coal miners) on p. 47 in: "Features: First Prize." *News Pictures of the Year 1951*. The Outstanding Photographs from the Eighth Annual News Pictures of the Year Competition and Exhibition jointly sponsored by Encyclopaedia Britannica Book of the Year and the University of Missouri School of Journalism. Edited by Clifton E. Edom. Louis Mariano, Publisher, Chicago, Ill. 1951. [96 pp.]

Photography Workshop

"Assignment in Studio 61. 12 Photographers: Smith." *Photography Workshop*, vol. 1, no. 3 (1951), pp. 28-29, 42. 21 b&w plus portrait.
[Issue of magazine turned over to 12 photographers' "interpretations" of one theme: a woman in a room with a bed and some other props. The photographers' results were then compared. Smith's model was Sunny Adams. He wrote a statement which is presented with the images.]

"After 7,500 Miles, a Wake." *Photography Workshop*, vol. 1, no. 3 (1951), pp. 34-35. 1 b&w (Spanish Village wake, son in door).
[Narrative episode of making wake photograph for Spanish Village.]

Semana (Madrid)

"De la Leyenda Negra a la Foto Negra Sobre España," by W. Fernandez Florez. *Semana* (Madrid), no. 596, 12th Year (July 1951), pp. 15-17. 6 b&w by Smith, 9 b&w by other photographers.
[Article protesting "Spanish Village" essay as being misrepresentative of the current Spanish economy. Has comparison photographs — mules vs. tractors — etc., taken by staff photographers of *Semana*.]

U.S. Camera

1 portrait, brief statement on p. 49 in: "U.S. Camera Achievement Awards." *U.S. Camera*, vol. 14, no. 12 (Dec. 1951), pp. 48-51.
[Smith won award for photo essay of year, "Spanish Village." Other awards went to Harold Edgerton, Robert Flaherty, Lejaren a Hiller, National Geographic Magazine, Thor Heyerdahl, Ansco Film Company, David White Company, Charles & Eugene Jones, and Emil Schulthess & Spuehler.]

U.S. Camera Annual

"A Spanish Village," by W. Eugene Smith. *U.S. Camera 1952*, (1951), pp. 149-159. 8 b&w.
[Another version of the "Spanish Village" essay, laid out by Smith with his own commentary about the photographs and about making the essay, stressing the threat of official harrassment.]

Who's Who in America. Monthly Supplement.

"Smith, W. Eugene," on p. 815 in: *The Monthly Supplement. A Current Adjunct to Who's Who in Amerca* (Aug. 1951).
[Brief biography.]